# Notes from Lebanon's First 200 Years
## Tennessee's City of Cedars

Copyright © 2019 by Sam Hatcher

All rights reserved. This book or any portion thereof may not be reproduced or used in any manner whatsoever without the express written permission of the publisher except for the use of brief quotations in a book review or scholarly journal.

First Printing: 2019

ISBN-13: 978-1-7334913-0-3

LCCN: 2019949213

For more information about this or other Grassleaf works, please visit grassleafpublishing.com or email info@grassleafpublishing.com.

## A note about Grassleaf Publishing

Grassleaf Publishing was created because of the belief that good literary works, films, music, and art of all types can come from anywhere and anyone. After all, all goodness comes from He who created goodness, and He is powerful enough to display that goodness through any individual.

As writing turned from a personal hobby into a passion, it was quickly realized that an author without a platform of thousands of followers has no chance to see his or her work published. This is disappointing to writers, but should also be disheartening to readers. What kind of good works are we missing out on?

Publishers will tell us that people do not read anymore. They blame the old-fashioned, boring art of reading. However, when one inspects the quality of books being printed, it is easy to see why consumers have turned away. Books are published based on the name of the author, not the quality of the content. Occasionally, a good book will make its way through, and readers will devour it over a weekend…especially young readers. So, it isn't the art of reading that's old-fashioned.

At Grassleaf Publishing, it is believed that good books can still be written. But the process of publishing must evolve. That's why Grassleaf operates differently than the traditional publishing company. Content and quality are the sole focus. The status, background, or life experience of an author doesn't matter. Grassleaf Publishing believes that if good content is made available, He will see that it serves its purpose.

As a reader, you may not recognize Grassleaf's authors, but hopefully you will recognize our logo and trust that it represents a worthwhile work.

Grassleaf Publishing was created to do one thing: contribute a verse.

Charles Brandon Wagoner
Founder, Grassleaf Publishing

# Notes from Lebanon's First 200 Years
## Tennessee's City of Cedars

**Sam Hatcher**

Dedicated to those who came before us

This history about the first 200 years of Lebanon, Tennessee's existence is dedicated to the men and women who have made this place such a wonderful community in which to live.

Those who lived here before us fought in wars, suffered through hard economic times, endured social change and through it all made Lebanon a stronger and better place that thrives with opportunity and is filled with a plentiful well of compassion.

It was the will of early settlers and the vision of those who followed that kept our town on course.

For that we should all be grateful.

And now for the next 200 years it will be our responsibility along with our children and their children and even those who follow them to keep our values in place and our town's progress marching forward.

# Table of Contents

**Foreword**
Preserving History — i

**Chapter One**
Measuring a Township's Greatness — 1

**Chapter Two**
Industrial Development Spurs City's Growth — 5

**Chapter Three**
Commerce Focused Around Public Square — 13

**Chapter Four**
Musical Notes — 29

**Chapter Five**
Weathering the Storms — 43

**Chapter Six**
Lebanon Puts Folks in Powerful Places — 55

**Chapter Seven**
Getting Here from There — 69

**Chapter Eight**
The Learning Process, Schools — 77

**Chapter Nine**
Those Who Healed the Community — 101

**Chapter Ten**
Potpourri — 117

**Chapter Eleven**
Which Would You Choose? — 145

**Acknowledgements** — 153

# Foreword
## Preserving History

Notes from Lebanon's First 200 Years

By my count as we near the final days of August - today is Thursday, August 29, 2019, and Labor Day will be Monday - there have been three very dense and heavy fogs. It is 4 o'clock in the morning as I write this and from the street lights in my neighborhood and what little bit of moonlight that remains I can see that this morning's fog will likely be just as thick as the two that fell on our city earlier this month.

So, why is that important in a book about Lebanon's 200 year history?

It's because years ago there was an "old saying" that the number of fogs in August would determine the number of snowfalls the coming winter would bring.

That may have been the case 40 years or so ago as you will read in the pages ahead but the weather records of recent history indicate that this age old accepted truth may no longer have value.

Whether it's global warming or just God's hand, Lebanon, at least in recent decades, has not received the great snowfalls as it once did many winters ago. From all indications from the sources researched, the last winters of multiple significant snows occurred in the late 1960s and early 1970s.

And this is why history is important.

History tells us about the past, how change has taken place, and prepares us for what we might expect in the years ahead.

It's not just about the weather.

But rather it's a record about how lives were changed by the introduction of industrial jobs, about the importance of education, about how hard work and a vision can influence an individual's future, and about how important it is to live in a community that cares about each other. And yes, it's about the weather too.

History also teaches us about past misdeeds, the mistreatment of others during the period of slavery and later during the time of segregation. History shows us when we erred in destroying a building that should have been preserved and makes us proud when we see a building kept intact that was deserving of restoration.

In many ways history speaks to us like a long lost relative.

It's like remembering what your father or grandfather told you about some happening long ago or maybe your mother sharing a favorite recipe passed down from one generation to another. These are treasures we don't want to forget. But, if not permanently preserved, they will be lost forever.

In this work, "Notes from Lebanon's First 200 Years," the effort has been made to capture and preserve much of the community's history. There will of course be oversights, places or happenings that should have been mentioned that weren't, and people who should have gotten "shout-outs" that didn't.

Please excuse these shortcomings but know that best intentions were at heart when composing the material.

We urge you to use this book as a catalyst to begin your own history. Tell your children about the importance of preserving memories and put on paper what you remember about what your parents and grandparents may have told you about a winter storm, their first experience of driving on the interstate, paying more than $4 for a gallon of gas, or seeing water sell for as much or more than milk.

This is the essence of history. If these matters, these remembrances are not kept, they will be lost forever.

It is the responsibility of all of us to make sure this doesn't happen.

# Chapter One
## Measuring a Township's Greatness

"To be sure, no piece of social machinery, however well constructed, can be effective unless there is back of it a will and a determination to make it work," words spoken by U.S. Secretary of State Cordell Hull in his Nobel Peace Prize Acceptance Speech in Oslo, Norway, on December 10, 1945.

A community, a township, a municipality is no greater than the contributions those have made who have lived within it bounds and have passed through its gates.

Judging the City of Lebanon by this axiom on measuring greatness, one would surely surmise that this once tiny village, whose charter of local government was created on October 27, 1819, has matured to become one of Tennessee's, the South's and perhaps the nation's, greatest of small town cities.

Much has happened and much has changed as Lebanon has prospered in good times, endured through hard times but has managed to survive all times.

The late Secretary Hull, who earned his law degree in Lebanon at Cumberland University, served the nation as Secretary of State during World War II.

He served in this post longer than any other before him or since and is regarded as the "father" of the United Nations.

Before being named Secretary of State, Secretary Hull represented Lebanon and Wilson County as the U.S. Representative for the 4th Congressional District and later as a U.S. Senator for Tennessee. The Nobel Prize recipient devoted much of his adult life to promoting and preserving world peace.

He's only one of many who have made so many contributions to our world as we know it today from beginnings here in the city named for the biblical land of cedars.

From Lebanon rubber o'rings for NASA rockets have been manufactured; a squad of college football players (mostly frat boys) was sent to Atlanta to play Georgia Tech and got whipped by a score of 222-0; two judges of the U.S. Supreme Court earned their law degrees; a mayor and later Lieutenant Governor initiated the idea of industrial subdivisions and industrial bonds so small communities could recruit industry; and a songwriter co-wrote one of the greatest country songs of all time.

## Measuring a Township's Greatness

For sure Lebanon has had and continues to have its day.

There have been extreme weather events, sightings of UFO's, hundreds of thousands of soldiers in training here, and many memorable occasions.

U.S. Senators, Members of Congress, governors and leaders in agriculture, business, education and the judiciary all earned their respective rights to passage, as the saying goes, in Lebanon, Tennessee.

Obviously, the quote attributed to Secretary Hull at the beginning of this passage refers to efforts required to sustain world peace.

A second quote for which he is also noted, "Never insult an alligator until after you have crossed the river," may just be a good general rule to follow as one wades through the trials and tribulations of life.

Whatever the case the history that has been forever etched in this town that once was just a village on a small stream of water and braced by a foundation of a hardened limestone bed is significant.

It's significant for a number of reasons but most importantly because it should make all of us proud who call this place our home.

Whether a resident moved here this year, last year, or has lived here all of their lives.

Whether they are second, third or fourth generation natives.

Or whether they came as a result of Amazon locating here, because they are employed with Bridgestone, or because they are an orthopedic surgeon at the local hospital.

There is good reason for all to be proud of Lebanon, the county seat of Wilson County. The community's first inhabitants chose to build their town on a site six miles north of the geographical center of the county, six miles south of the Cumberland River and at the fork of two creeks.

In the pages that follow a historical overview will be presented examining Lebanon's first 200 years.

Personalities, events, commercial development, and other topics of importance will get a nod.

# Chapter Two
## Industrial Development Spurs City's Growth

Lebanon's industrial development has seen a number of twists and turns throughout the town's first 200 years.

Before 1900 the town's economic strength and industrial base was based on a strong agricultural heritage. Folk who lived in Lebanon during the early and mid-1800s were crop farmers, dairymen, and horse traders and trainers.

During this period Lebanon and Wilson County earned a reputation as one of the state's leading agricultural centers and for that reason whatever industries existed and provided jobs, they did so because of agriculture.

These places of work might include flour or grain milling, processing of livestock, shearing and capturing wool from sheep and refining it into material, and other similar or related businesses that provided job opportunities.

There was a broad diversification of crops farmed near Lebanon including acres of cotton, corn and wheat, and an equal diversification of livestock that included sheep, hogs, cattle, and horses.

Although fields of cotton are generally no longer found locally, Wilson County at one time had a number of cotton gins and, while cotton may not have been "King" as in West Tennessee, it did have a place here.

According to the "History of Wilson County" published in 1961, an acre of local farm land in 1870 cost about $20. Today, 2019, that same acre, but no longer farm land, in the city of Lebanon can cost as much as several hundred thousand dollars.

In a report filed by the City of Lebanon in 1984 and titled a General

Development Plan, city officials in the administration of Mayor Willis H. (Tex) Maddox, discussing the history of the city's economic growth, state that in the early 1800s "Lebanon was noted as a center of horse breeding and racing, and later as a major stagecoach center."

Ironically some 200 years later, albeit not a stagecoach center any longer, the town continues to attribute much of its economic strength to a number of major transportation arteries, a local airport capable of accommodating jet aircraft, the first commuter rail system in modern times in Tennessee, and Lebanon's closeness in proximity to Nashville's international airport.

*Postcard of Historic Lebanon Square.*

When considering the "whys" behind Lebanon's industrial and commercial growth in recent years, accessibility to valuable transportation options capable of connecting the local community to many of the population centers east of the Mississippi River within a matter of hours has no doubt been a major contributing factor.

In 1908 Lebanon got its first taste of how a manufacturing plant can change a small town when the Lebanon Woolen Mills, owned by a group

## Industrial Development Spurs City's Growth

of local businessmen, opened its facility a couple of blocks from the Public Square on North Maple Street.

After the start of the Woolen Mills other industries began to find their place in Lebanon.

Barry-Carter Milling Co., located on South Cumberland Street about a block off the Public Square, launched its start in Lebanon in 1929. Following World War II, Barry-Carter became a division of Martha White Flour and the facility today operates as Shenandoah Mills.

In 1936 yet another manufacturing plant was added to Lebanon's industrial landscape: the Lebanon Garment Plant. It too was located about a block off the Public Square on East Market Street.

*The Lebanon Woolen Mills founded in 1908.*

Perhaps no single person had as much impact on industrial growth in Lebanon, and for that matter in the Volunteer State, as the late William D. Baird, a former city mayor and Lieutenant Governor of Tennessee.

Baird had a vision to help enable small towns like Lebanon to be able to attract industry and to compete with the state's larger cities and also with cities and communities in other states.

He created a first-of-a-kind industrial park for the state of Tennessee in Lebanon. It was a unique idea he generated in his role as mayor.

Known today as the William D. Baird Industrial Subdivision, the industrial park contains some 278 acres.

The first industry to be recruited to the new subdivision especially designed for industry with city paved streets, all utilities, and frontage with rail connections was the Hartmann Luggage Company in 1956. Hartmann built a manufacturing facility on acreage at the corner of Hartmann Drive and the Baddour Parkway.

Baird, an alumnus of Cumberland University and former chairman of the school's Board of Trust, held that if Lebanon was going to grow and prosper, there had to be an adequate employment base and a means to support the city's current and future needs through property tax revenue.

The recruitment of industry did both.

*Billboard recognizes William D. Baird industrial subdivision on Baddour Parkway.*

It provided new resources to increase tax revenue and opened up new job opportunities for those already living here and for their generations to come. And new industry brought new residents to Lebanon who consequently built homes here and contributed to the local economy.

Baird also played a key role in influencing the state legislature to pass the Industrial Building Bond Act Of 1955, which allows local government to issue industrial bonds by pledging only the rental income from the business.

This was proven to give small towns and counties a serious advantage in being able to recruit industry across the state as now they would have a mechanism in place to offer funding as an incentive to an industry desiring to relocate.

As mayor of Lebanon, Baird focused much of his efforts on recruiting industry.

On his watch the Texas Boot Company was created here in 1951 by a German immigrant, Harry Vise, who with his family narrowly escaped persecution by Nazi troops before coming to America penny-less.

A number of other industries either relocated here or expanded existing operations during this time.

A second early company to build a manufacturing facility on the eastern edge of Baird Subdivision in the 1960s and remains here still today was the TRW-Ross Gear, Steering Gear Division. For many years TRW (ZF Industries) held the distinction of being the city's largest employer.

The Precision Rubber Company, now closed, built a large manufacturing plant on Hartmann Drive, employed as many as 600 workers at one time and manufactured rubber o'rings for various products and industries, including the NASA space program.

Some of the other companies to locate in the industrial park included Lebanon Aluminum, Steve's Sash and Door, the K.O. Lester Company, Bay's Bread, Custom Packaging, Lebanon Wire Products, Fortune Plastics, Rock City Box (later Rock-Tenn), Custom Specialty, Midwesco, and Bradley Candy Company.

In 1978, Toshiba America, a manufacturer of televisions and microwave ovens, was added to the list of those occupying the Baird Subdivision.

Toshiba, a Japanese owned company, became the city's largest manufacturing employer with more than 650 employees and grew its original plant size from 148,000 sq. ft. to approximately one million sq. ft.

*A worker helps assemble a new Toshiba television.*

before announcing just over two decades from when it arrived that it would be closing and abandoning its operations here.

Since then the Toshiba building has been acquired by a private investor and has been reconfigured to house a number of individual companies, some of which are manufacturing companies.

As many as 7,000 jobs existed in the 1960s in the Baird Industrial Subdivision.

Today Cracker Barrel Old Country Store, Inc. maintains a headquarters campus there.

LoJac, a locally owned paving and building materials company, was located in the subdivision and subsequently after two companies, Vulcan Materials and Alley-Cassetty, in separate acquisitions purchased LoJac's operations in recent years, both have continued a presence in the subdivision.

As the Baird Subdivision neared capacity, city leaders began looking for other areas, tracts of land, that may be suitable to establish more parks specifically designated for industry.

The newer industrial parks include South Perimeter Industrial Park with industries Lifeway, Performance Food Group, Royal Canin (Nutro Products), Georgia Pacific, Lochinvar, and L & W Engineering; Commerce Farms Park with industries Bridgestone/Firestone, Carlex, and XPO Logistics; Cherry Farm Park with industries American Wonder Porcelain and Kenwall Steel; Park 840 Park with industries Amazon, Permobil, Leviton, Maplehurst Bakeries, and O'Reillys Logistics Center;

## Industrial Development Spurs City's Growth

Park 840 East Park with GEODIS (Starbucks); East Gate Park with CEVA Logistics, FedEx Supply Chain, Manheim Auto Auction, OPTORO, REMAR and Communications Test Designs; and Highway Industrial Park which includes Builders First Source.

While some of these may edge just over the bounds of the city limits of Lebanon, they are all generally accepted as being Lebanon industries.

Much of the credit for the recruitment of new industry and business to Lebanon and the two other county municipalities, Watertown and Mt. Juliet, in recent years is given to the Joint Economic and Community Development Board of Wilson County.

The JECDB, formed in 1989 as a quasi-government entity, is staffed by professionals who are expertly trained and educated in the field of economic and community development or, in layman terms, in seeking out and recruiting industry and commercial enterprise.

G.C. Hixson is the current executive director of the JECDB and Tammy Stokes is assistant executive director.

Lebanon's industrial workforce has multiplied to the point that the town's population is said to swell more than 40 percent during daylight hours as employees report to work from a number of nearby towns and counties.

*Major employers in Lebanon in 2019 with employee count*
    Cracker Barrel – 820
    Performance Food Group – 646
    CEVA Logistics – 625
    TRW – 500
    Manheim Auto Auction – 425
    Lochinvar - 425

# Chapter Three
## Commerce Focused Around Public Square

The Lebanon-Wilson County Chamber of Commerce, organized in 1924, would advise the city's steady growth; its rise to a top tier ranking in household income; its low unemployment rate and continually expanding industrial base; and its closeness in proximity to a number of smaller towns some 20 minutes or so away have all contributed significantly to a robust local economy.

In early 2019 Wilson County was declared Tennessee's fastest growing county and its second wealthiest, two important statistics that help explain

*The southeast quadrant of the Lebanon Square is shown in this 1890's photo. There is a well in the lower right center of the photo and an electric pole on the left.*

why commerce here continues on an upward trend.

New restaurants, retailers, added chain stores, and some unusual additions maybe never seen here before until a few years ago like tattoo shops, all speak to the city's vibrant economy.

The late Dr. Frank Burns, a journalist, author, teacher, and county historian, reports in the "History of Wilson County" that the first store in Lebanon was opened in 1803 by William Allen, an Irishman. And a year later Andrew Jackson and his wife's nephew, John Hutchings, opened a second business here, Jackson and Hutchings.

Businesses continued to sprout as more and more began to populate the area.

The Texas war hero Sam Houston opened his law office on East Main Street in 1818.

And for awhile during the 1820s, Lebanon was recognized as a center or supply point for the Southwest. It was also during this time that hotels and boarding houses began a presence here.

As merchants came to town and businesses continued to be developed, homes and commercial structures were erected. Many of the structures were built with slave labor.

Accounts of new businesses opening and Lebanon continuing down a path to become a trade and merchandise center are told in Goodspeed Publishing Company's, History of Tennessee, Nashville 1887.

In the 1850s, Goodspeed reports that a Colonel John Price, a reputable stage coach operator, opened the first department store in Lebanon selling everything from men's and women's fashions to even a side of beef. Shortly after opening his store he bought out another merchant and later acquired several of the town's existing businesses. According to Burns' writing, Price owned all the town's stores except a drug store, barrooms, and butcher shop.

This early Lebanon business tycoon soon became overwhelmed with his acquisitions and the demand they required of his time and he sold each of them one-by-one.

Goodspeed also notes that a dry goods and grocery store was established in 1865 by a Clark Cook and his partner, a Mr. McCarty. Their new business brought the first goods to Lebanon following the Civil War.

*Mule Day sale on Lebanon's Square in the late 1890s.*

While a few retail stores opened in Lebanon during the early and mid-1800s, several hotels were established including the Baird Hotel on the northwest corner of the Public Square, John W. Comer's hotel on the corner of West Market Street and North Cumberland, the Watkins House a block south of Comer's hotel, a hotel operated by Jim Jackson on the corner of Gay Street and South Cumberland, and the West Side Hotel on the corner of South Maple Street and West Main.

The West Side Hotel, which was a prominent structure for many years in Lebanon, was destroyed by fire in 1982. Among many of its unique early features was what is described as an opera house on the hotel's second floor.

The need for hotels and boardinghouses grew during this period as Lebanon's commercial interests expanded.

*Cattle drive down West Main Street in late 1800s.*

Visitors coming to Lebanon to buy or sell goods, members of the judiciary, politicians, traveling preachers, and others would often come from towns 20 to 30 miles away. Their journey to Lebanon represented a day's ride by horse or stagecoach and required an overnight stay thus encouraging the need for hotels.

Lebanon's commercial enterprises continued to expand through the late 1800s and past the nation's entry into World War I.

Perhaps the oldest store front still open today for business in Lebanon with the same name on its signage is the Fakes and Hooker Lumber Company.

## Commerce Focused Around Public Square

*Site of Fakes and Hooker Lumber and Coal Company on South Maple Street in 1867 where the business is still located.*

Remaining an independently owned business and still with an address on South Maple Street, Fakes and Hooker got its start more than 150 years ago in 1867.

Wilson County Motors is another business listed among the city's oldest that continues to be open today.

The car dealership opened in 1927 on South Maple Street, a block off Lebanon's Square. It moved to West Main Street in 1964, where it now hosts a Hyundai dealership. The auto company also has a second location for its Chevrolet, Buick, GMC franchise on South Hartmann Drive.

Winstead P. Bone, Jr., in partnership with A. W. Hooker, founded Wilson County Motors. The dealership continues to be owned by members of the Bone family.

W.P. Bone, III, who heads the business now, notes that at its original location the dealership survived a major fire, several floods, war, and the Great Depression. In 1933, in the heart of the Depression, the dealership's total profit for the year was reported at just over $400.

Donald Philpot was the Ford dealer in Lebanon during this time frame. The first Lebanon car dealer was Graham and Seale, which sold Model T Fords. The first gas station was opened in 1920 by W.C. Clay.

Two local dairies, Perfection Dairy and

*Tucker's Cafe just off the Lebanon Square advertised on a handbill in 1933 breakfast for a nickel.*

*Lebanon Boosters hold celebration on the Square in 1910.*

Johnson's Dairy, provided dairy products to the town from the 1940s forward. Their service, of course, included home delivery.

In the 1940s the town saw the opening of McDowell Tire Store that later would evolve into the McDowell Cadillac, Oldsmobile, Rambler/American Motors dealership.

Also during this era Hankins and Smith and later Hankins Byars and Jewel opened a service station, oil distribution company, and became the town's Pontiac dealer.

Much of the credit for Lebanon's strength in commerce is now and has always been directly related to a strong and competitive banking community.

As far back as 1820 Lebanon has had a number of banks competing locally for commercial business.

When Gov. William Bowen Campbell left office in 1853, he returned to Lebanon to be president of the Bank of Middle Tennessee. However, already present in the town was the Bank of the State of Tennessee and shortly after the Civil War People's National Bank was organized here.

Today there are five local community banks in Lebanon with local boards of directors. That list includes CedarStone Bank, First Freedom Bank, Liberty State Bank, Southern Bank of Tennessee, and Wilson Bank and Trust.

Besides these financial institutions, there are also branch offices here representing First Tennessee, Bank of America, Capital Bank, Pinnacle,

# Commerce Focused Around Public Square

*Construction was begun in 1914 on Lebanon's old Post Office now the offices of the Wilson County Election Commission. The building was completed 18 months later in 1915.*

Regions, F&M Bank, BankTennessee, and SunTrust Bank.

And there are two major credit unions serving the market, including Old Hickory Credit Union and US Community Credit Union.

Four of the existing community banks were started by veterans of the banking community who had previous employment engagements at other local banks. The late J. Roy Wauford had a large stake of ownership and kept management reins on Liberty State Bank until a majority interest in

*Late 1960s aerial photo of downtown Lebanon business district.*

the bank was sold to Citizens Bank in Lafayette in 1999. Citizens Bank acquired the remaining outstanding stock of Liberty State Bank in 2013. Liberty State Bank originated in DeKalb County. Wauford was responsible for bringing the bank to Lebanon.

Randall Clemons left Peoples Bank (acquired by SunTrust) to start Wilson Bank and Trust. Bob McDonald, previously the local head of SunTrust Bank's Wilson County operations, is credited with launching CedarStone Bank. Ken Howell, John Lancaster and John Bradshaw, all three formerly with First Tennessee Bank, led the effort to open First Freedom Bank. David Major and Sam Short, who led the organization of two other local banks, are responsible for starting Southern Bank of Tennessee.

Lebanon Bank, with roots dating as far back as 1884, was organized in 1951 by a group of local businessmen who acquired Lebanon Bank and Trust Company. Lebanon Bank was bought by First Tennessee Bank in 1987. Its first office was on the southeast corner of the Public Square where the law offices of Lannom and Williams are today.

People's Bank, originally organized in 1915 to serve the community of Norene in southeast Wilson County, was reorganized in 1967 by a

*Original Wilson County Courthouse.*

## Commerce Focused Around Public Square

group of local investors and brought to Lebanon as a community bank. The bank was acquired in 1986 by Third National Bank that later became SunTrust Bank.

The focal point of Lebanon's retail business until the early to mid-1950s was the town's Public Square and one or two blocks off the Square.

There were some exceptions however including two prominent grocery stores, Mosers, originally on South Maple Street and later on Baddour Parkway, and "big and little" Eskews on West Main. Eskews, which delivered groceries in a dark blue panel truck for decades, had two locations. The store's customers assigned the "big" and "little" tag lines to the two stores located only a couple of blocks apart on West Main Street.

Retailers, restaurants, barrooms, lawyer offices and other businesses and store fronts were all found on or very near the Public Square.

Their existence on the Square was not by happenstance.

The Square, for more than 75 years from Lebanon's beginning, was the city's center of commerce activity.

*Lebanon Fire Department in late 1950s.*

It was where the main spring was that provided water to the community; where the county courthouse was located until 1966; where the county jail was; where the city police and fire departments were until the early 1960s; and where city hall was. If you had business in Lebanon, the Public Square was likely to be your destination.

The list of stores and retail shops that have operated on or around the Square is expansive. Some were there for a couple of years while others maintained their presence for decades.

Hardware stores were plentiful around the Square as were dry goods retailers, pharmacies, and some restaurants and places to drink a beer.

Hard liquor was not permitted. Although, if you knew the right white frame house just two blocks or so north of the Square, you could buy a pint or shot of a favorite whiskey.

Beer parlors and barrooms were dotted around the Square, mostly on the north side, so that they would be near the police station, located at the corner of West Market and North Cumberland, just in case trouble broke out.

One particular area of the Square, the northwest corner, was known for a longtime as "the Devil's Elbow," because of a couple of beer parlors being located there.

From the early to mid-1900s forward some of the longer standing stores and businesses around the Square included M.D. Steele Hardware (a block off South Cumberland Street), S.N. Cook Hardware, Cox's Furniture and Gifts (now relocated a block off the Square on West Main, Bellar Furniture Store, Johnson's Furniture, McClain and Smith (men's clothing), Draper and Darwin (dry goods), Cowan's Department Store, Askew and Grissom, later John Hatcher's Clothing (men's clothing), Mack and Jim's (boys and men's wear), McAdoo's (lady's wear), Bradshaw Drugs, Shannon's Drug Store, National Drug Store, Welty's Five and Dime, Kuhn's 10-Cent Store, H.G. Hills Grocery, Ideal Cafe (formerly the Orange Bar), Tucker's City Cafe, Barbara's (women's clothing), The Daisy Shop, Davis Dress Shop,

*Lebanon police officers uncover a whiskey still inside the city limits.*

## Commerce Focused Around Public Square

Princess Theatre, Capitol Theatre, Dollar Store, Ideal Barber Shop, Modern Barbershop, Westside Barbershop, Lebanon Bank, Commerce Union Bank, Kroger (a block off the Square on College Street), Simms (televisions and electronics first in a small shop on College Street then in the building previously occupied by Kroger), Hill Feeds (South Maple Street), Hinson Tire Store then Goodyear Tire Store (South Maple Street), Sorrel's Pharmacy (College Street), and Chastain's Shoe Shop (shoe repair), Seats Studio, Cooksey Bros. Hardware, Independent Drugs, Pool Hall, Kirkpatrick's Shoes (now Markham's Shoe Store), 0900 Taxi Stand (0900 was the phone number), Cedar City Machine Shop, Rose's 10-Cent Store, Eskew's Grocery, and Baird and Safely Hardware.

The Square lost a bit of its appeal for retail business when the courthouse closed and was torn down and a new courthouse opened and when retail strip centers began to spring-up across the city.

*The 1897 photo is of a popcorn party hosted by Bob Weir at his store on Lebanon's Public Square. Among those attending are Bob Weir (second from left), Amzi Hooker (to the right of Weir) and others unidentified.*

# Notes from Lebanon's First 200 Years

*Past presidents of the Lebanon-Wilson County Chamber of Commerce gathered for a group photo in 1994. (Front row) John Hatcher, Comer Donnell, Bill Bell, Jesse Coe, J.B. Leftwich, Randal Clemmons, Bob Van Hooser. (Second row) Don McDougle, Bill McDowell, Tony Shipp, Max Smith, Nelson Steed, David Foutch, Jim Lancaster. (Back row) Jim Mills, Mike Baker, Don Simpson, Ted Aulds, Charles Bradley, Wendell Kopp, Ed Callis.*

## Lebanon Wilson County Chamber of Commerce
### PAST PRESIDENTS & CHAIRMEN OF THE BOARD

| | | |
|---|---|---|
| 1924 W.D. FERRELL | 1956 MR. E.O. JACKSON | 1988 NELSON STEED |
| 1925 W.D. FERRELL | 1957 BILL REGEN | 1989 BILL McDOWELL |
| 1926 O.B. CLEVELAND | 1958 ROY CRIPS | 1990 TONY SHIPP |
| 1927 EDWARD GRAHAM | 1959 JIM LANCASTER | 1991 DAVID FOUTCH |
| 1928 EDWARD GRAHAM | 1960 DR. B.S. HOWARD | 1992 JIM MILLS |
| 1929 STARK GOODBAR | 1961 TED EZELL | 1993 MIKE BAKER - deceased |
| 1930 HERMAN ESKEW | 1962 KEN LESTER JR. | 1994 DON McDOUGLE |
| 1931 HERMAN ESKEW | 1963 ROBERT VANHOOSER | 1995 KEN HOWELL |
| 1932 KERLEY WILSON | 1964 HUBERT TURNER | 1996 PAT BONE |
| 1933 ROY CRIPS | 1965 JOHN HATCHER | 1997 MARK LEE |
| 1934 KERLEY WILSON | 1966 GRAYDON ROBINSON | 1998 JACKIE GAITHER |
| 1935 KERLEY WILSON | 1967 JESSE COE | 1999 DAVE WHITE |
| 1936 ROY CRIPS | 1968 LOUIS SMARTT | 2000 PAUL STOVALL |
| 1937 ROY CRIPS | 1969 W.L. BELL JR. | 2001 BOB McDONALD |
| 1938 ROY CRIPS | 1970 COMER A. DONNELL | 2002 BOB LEE |
| 1939 W.J. BAIRD | 1971 CECIL J. JOHNSON SR. | 2003 JUDGE BARRY TATUM |
| 1940 W.J. BAIRD | 1972 CHARLES P. BRADLEY | 2004 JOHN McDEARMAN |
| 1941 HOMER SHANNON | 1973 DON SIMPSON | 2005 KEN CALDWELL |
| 1942 W.C. CLAY | 1974 DARWIN LANKFORD | 2006 ERIC THOMPSON |
| 1943 A.A. ADAMS JR. | 1975 WENDELL R. KOPP | 2007 PAUL C. STUMB IV |
| 1944 O.B. CLEVELAND | 1976 ROGER E. BEATTY | 2008 BECKY JENNINGS |
| 1945 A.A. ADAMS JR. | 1977 E.H. McCLINTOCK | 2009 JOHN LANCASTER |
| 1946 A.A. ADAMS JR. | 1978 J.W. "BILL" MARTIN | 2010 DANNY STEWART |
| 1947 A.A. ADAMS JR. | 1979 ED CALLIS | 2011 PAUL JEWELL |
| 1948 HARRELL MEADORS | 1980 J.B. LEFTWICH | 2012 CHRIS CROWELL |
| 1949 W.H. MADDOX | 1981 BILL McDOWELL | 2013 RICK SMITH |
| 1950 J.D. DRAPER | 1982 JERRY FRANKLIN | 2014 JOHN BRYAN |
| 1951 ROY CRIPS | 1983 MAX SMITH - deceased | 2015 JOHN BRADSHAW |
| 1952 JIM HORN HANKINS | 1984 RANDALL CLEMONS | 2016 SCOTT JASPER |
| 1953 HOYAL JOHNSON | 1985 RICHARD MACON | 2017 JUD NAVE |
| 1954 HOYAL JOHNSON | 1986 TED R. AULDS | 2018 JB OWENS |
| 1955 CHARLES LOYD | 1987 JERE McCULLOUCH – deceased | 2019 NECOLE BELL |

## Commerce Focused Around Public Square

One of the first strip centers to open was Cedars Shopping Center on West Main Street in 1956. Merchants included Modern Men's Shop, which had previously been located on East Main Street near the Square; Winkler's Drug Store; Winfrey's Rone Jewelry; and Ben Franklin's Five and Dime, previously Welty's which was located on the Square.

There were two out buildings constructed in association with the shopping center. One, a larger structure, was occupied by H.G. Hills, which had moved to the new building from its store on the Square, and the other was a smaller building at the rear of the center where Lebanon Bank put a branch office and Lebanon's first drive-up window for customer service.

After the Cedars Center opened, other strip centers popped-up on virtually all sides of Lebanon. These shopping areas held some local stores but mostly became places where regional and national chains would locate.

The Outlets Shopping Mall on Lebanon's south side near I-40 began to open stores in the mid-2000s and brought yet another new shopping experience to the community featuring significant discounts from a number of nationally recognized retail stores.

About the same time, Walmart introduced to Lebanon a Super Walmart store, closing its original location in a strip center west of town where Big Lots is located today.

Soon stores began to drift from the Square. Many closed. And the Public Square took on a new identity. Lebanon became known as the "Antique Capital of the South," and the Square and several of the buildings a block or two blocks off the Square were now antique stores and mixed-in were a few antique consignment businesses. Cuz's Antiques and Downtown Antique Mall were the main staples for many years to the Square's antique reputation.

In the mid and late 2000s the Public Square saw and is continuing to see more change.

Bob and Pam Black purchased and totally rehabilitated the Capitol Theatre restoring it back to much of its original decor. The Capitol regularly presents live musical productions, viewing events, theatrical plays and other programs.

The Capitol was a first step in bringing new life to the Public Square. Since its opening in 2010, new boutique retail shops have opened on the Square along with a popular coffee destination, the Split Bean, and a new eatery, Town Social.

Law offices continue to have a strong presence on the Square.

As the saying is quoted, "what goes around – comes around," and Lebanon's Public Square is no exception. It's seen change after change and continues to be a viable part of Lebanon's economy.

*Construction Causes Labor Shortages*

In the 1960s TVA acquired land on the Cumberland River between Carthage and Hartsville to build a nuclear power plant. Less than 10 years after construction on the plant was begun and several millions of dollars had been spent, TVA stopped construction and canceled its plans for the facility offering that the future need for electric power had been grossly over estimated.

During the period of construction hundreds from Lebanon and other nearby communities rushed to the project for jobs. Hourly wages paid workers by TVA were more than twice what others in the market were being paid.

The impact on the local labor force and local economy was significant. Laborers, skilled and otherwise, rushed to the TVA plant for jobs, making for a shortage of skilled workers and tradesmen elsewhere. But for the local economy, the TVA plant's construction served as a major boost.

## Commerce Focused Around Public Square

*The photo is of a barn on Old Hartsville Pike just a short distance from Lebanon. The cooling tower in the background makes for an interesting blend of old and new. The photo was shot by the late Bill Cook, chief photographer for The Lebanon Democrat.*

# Chapter Four
## Musical Notes

Lebanon's library of contributions to music crisscrosses all generations and virtually all genres.

In more recent times the town has provided prime locations for a number of music videos from some of music's most popular artists.

On more than one occasion Cumberland University has been a host site for music videos that featured among others Reba McEntire and Taylor Swift. But also filming videos in Lebanon have been Keith Urban, Miranda Lambert, and Kid Rock.

While much of Lebanon's history with music involves country music, there are exceptions.

The listing of performers and artists found in this chapter may not necessarily be a compilation of all the names of those from or connected to Lebanon who have made contributions to this particular area of the arts, but, as the list appears, it is an impressive class.

*Paul McCartney and the Wings summer visit*

The most memorable exception to country music happenings in Lebanon would likely be the summer Paul McCartney, his wife Linda, and his band "Wings" gathered in Lebanon renting the home of the late Curly and Bernice Putman for a stay of several weeks.

Although "Beetle Mania" had passed by this time, the fan rage and curiosity in 1974 about Paul McCartney was as vibrant and exciting as ever.

McCartney sightings were reported throughout the summer as he and his bandmates would be spotted at local markets restocking beer inventory, picking-up sandwich fixings, or shopping for other necessities.

The stay in Lebanon provided McCartney and his band the opportunity to record a number of tunes on Music Row in Nashville. One song they recorded, "Junior's Farm," a number three hit in the fall of 1974, is said to be a tribute to the time they spent at the Putman residence.

*Paul McCartney and friends pose for a photo in 1974 on the front porch of the Curly and Bernice Putman home on Franklin Road near Lebanon.*

### Curly Putman's "Green Grass"

The name Curly Putman is memorable in and of itself as this Hall of Fame songwriter who made his home in Lebanon literally gave the world a collection of music that will be remembered forever.

Of the hundreds he wrote there are two songs for which Putman is always linked, "Green, Green Grass of Home," and "He Stopped Loving Her Today," a tune he co-wrote with Bobby Braddock.

Few songs, if any, have been recorded by as many artists and in as many languages as "Green, Green Grass of Home." The world has been listening to this ballad since it was first recorded in 1965.

Among those who have recorded "Green Grass," as Putman and

# Musical Notes

those in the business would frequently refer to the classic, are Porter Wagoner, Del Reeves, Bobby Bare, Charley Pride, Gene Parsons, The Statler Brothers, Jerry Lee Lewis, Roger Miller, Dean Martin, Johnny Cash, Frankie Laine, Merle Haggard, Hank Snow, George Jones, Trini Lopez, Joan Baez, The Grateful Dead, Elvis Presley, Kenny Rogers and others.

*Curly Putman, "Write 'em sad – sing 'em lonesome" album cover.*

"He Stopped Loving Her Today," released in 1980, has been named in several surveys as the greatest country song of all time. It was first recorded by George Jones and was named song of the year by the Country Music Association in 1980 and 1981.

*Lebanon's local radio*

While there have been several from Lebanon to be successful songwriters and performers in the music industry, there's been only one commercial venture here to serve as a means for the general public to hear their contributions.

In 1949, a license was granted for a 250-watt commercial radio station to be located in Lebanon and operated as WCOR AM 900.

Owned by Warren Gilpin, the station's studio was located on the Lebanon Public Square and its transmitter tower on Trousdale Ferry Pike, where the station, tower, and its studios are currently located.

The call letters WCOR were established as an acronym of sorts for Wilson County's Only Radio.

In the early days the station was the first voice of news in Wilson County. It was also where locals could get up-to-date obituary reports and tune-in to hear the daily "Birthday Club," a broadcast listing of local names celebrating birthdays on that day.

Throughout its history WCOR and in recent years its sister station, WANT FM, have provided the area with programming devoted largely to the country music genre as well as news reports, informative interview programs, and sports coverage of local high schools, Cumberland University, the Tennessee Titans, and others.

First airing in 1993, WANT FM has a signal strength that dominates Wilson County and is capable of capturing audiences in portions of Davidson, Sumner, Trousdale, Smith, DeKalb, Rutherford and Cannon counties.

Throughout its history the station has realized a number of changes in ownership. As mentioned, the first owner and founder was Warren Gilpin. Two others who operated the station as partners for several years beginning in the 1950s were Ted Ezell and Jack Hendrickson.

Until being purchased and operated by its current owner, Susie James, and a group of investment partners in 1993, the station struggled through some difficult periods that eventually led to it going off-the-air for several years.

Not long after James and her partners acquired the station she made the decision to buy them out and became the sole owner. Once acquired by James, significant changes were made and both WANT FM and WCOR AM became and have continued to be viable and credible broadcast entities.

Much of the owner's interest in the radio business she readily admits was developed by her stepfather the late William O. (Bill) Barry, who owned several radio stations himself and was somewhat of an icon in the industry.

A general overview of programming for WANT FM 98.9 and WCOR AM 1490 is described by management as featuring a "Real Country" format, blending a traditional sound of today's hottest new artists, with the greatest country classics.

Familiar on-air personalities include Coleman Walker, who has a morning interview show, "Coleman and Company"; M.J. Lucas, who manages disc jockey and announcing duties along with some morning game shows; and Fred Anthony Burton, known best to his listeners as "Fantastic Fred," who does a regular Saturday night program with a mix of rhythm and blues, soul, disco, rock and roll and some modern hip-hop.

*His career in radio started in World War II*

An influence on the radio industry in Tennessee and nationally for decades, an owner of several radio stations, and an enthusiast and promoter of the "big band sound" was the late William O. (Bill) Barry, a "Legacy" member of the Tennessee Association of Broadcasters Hall of Fame.

Barry's family name was associated with several Lebanon businesses including the prominent Barry-Carter Milling Co., which after World War II became a business division of Martha White Flour.

His legendary career in broadcasting began shortly after he enlisted in the Army at age 18 during World War II as much of his time in uniform was spent with the 13th Armored Division, as a radio operator in a Tank Battalion. During the war he was deployed to the European theater serving initially in France and later in Austria.

A graduate of Castle Heights Military Academy and Vanderbilt University, Barry, who developed an interest in the "big band sound" of dance music while in high school, organized his own cadet orchestra and played at several of the Heights' formal dances. He did the same as a student at Vanderbilt with his student orchestra performing at a number of university dances and social events.

It was when he returned to Lebanon after the war, that he began his accredited career in the radio and broadcasting industry. While still a student at Vanderbilt, he attempted to secure an AM radio station for Lebanon and at the time was working on-air at WGNS radio in

Murfreesboro.

His first acquisition in the business came in 1957 when he and a business partner purchased WSOK-FM in Nashville later changing the call letters of the station to WFMB. In 1965 the station was sold to the Life and Casualty Insurance Company which subsequently changed its call letters to WLAC-FM.

Barry, who played a key role in launching Nashville's public radio station, WPLN-FM, maintained ownership interests in a number of Nashville area stations including WAMB, WMAK, and WZEZ.

He is also credited with helping others acquire radio stations and licenses among those his stepdaughter Susie James, who owns and operates Lebanon stations WANT-FM and WCOR-AM.

Remembered for his knowledge of the business from the microphone to the engineering room, Barry in 1994 was presented the Tennessee Association of Broadcasters "Distinguished Service Award," the organization's highest honor. His accomplishments were again recognized in 2012 when the Tennessee Radio Hall of Fame presented him its first "Lifetime Achievement Award."

Frequently active in community events and charitable causes, he believed an education to be a precious gift and supported public education as well as Cumberland University and Friendship Christian School.

*Charlie Daniels sends Devil to Georgia*

It's a bit of a reach to connect Charlie Daniels to Lebanon as he prefers to claim Mt. Juliet as his hometown but truth be known his farm on Central Pike is about as close to the Lebanon city limits now after years of annexation as it is Mt. Juliet.

And besides that Daniels holds an Honorary Doctorate Degree from Lebanon's Cumberland University for his contributions to education and for many years he'd slip away from the tour bus for afternoons of golf at Lebanon's Five Oaks Country Club where he and his wife Hazel are still members.

Daniels, a heralded songwriter and multi-instrument performer, is perhaps known best for his riveting, fiddle playing number-one country hit "The Devil Went Down to Georgia," although he's had many other successes.

He was inducted into the Cheyenne Frontier Days Hall of Fame in 2002, the Grand Ole Opry in 2008, the Musicians Hall of Fame and Museum in 2009, and the Country Music Hall of Fame in 2016.

*Country Music Hall of Fame's Charlie Daniels strums a guitar.*

*David Corlew keeping Charlie Daniels popular*

Charlie Daniels would likely be the first to say that success in the music business doesn't just happen. There are strategies, business acumen, industry relations, and other matters that blend to make an entertainer or performer successful and popular for a significant number of years. David Corlew has been that person for Charlie Daniels and the Charlie Daniels Band since 1973.

Corlew, who lives with his talented wife Carolyn, a singer with the Charlie Daniels Band and former Ms. Senior America, on a farm near Lebanon, is president and CEO of Blue Hats Records and a past president of the Academy of Country Music.

He has been the recipient of a number of prestigious industry awards and is a co-founder along with Daniels of The Journey Home Project, an organization formed to aid veterans by helping connect them with not-for-profit causes that provide rehabilitation, reintegration, and opportunities as they transition to civilian life.

Notes from Lebanon's First 200 Years

*Lebanon brothers discover Flatt and Scruggs*

One of Lebanon's more fascinating stories related to the music industry is how the Bluegrass duo Flatt and Scruggs was discovered and subsequently put in the limelight by two brothers from Lebanon selling flour.

The late Homer and Efford Burke were traveling in East Tennessee near Knoxville for their employer Barry Carter Milling Company, a manufacturer of Martha White flour, when the two happened upon a performance by Lester Flatt and Earl Scruggs.

At their insistence to executives at Martha White Flour (Martha White was a major sponsor of WSM's Grand Ole Opry at the time), Flatt and Scruggs were invited to appear on the popular radio show. From there the Bluegrass duo streaked to fame.

*Maude Woodfork McElroy named Aunt Jemima*

Although she is not remembered for her musical talents despite winning a radio marathon in California by singing and performing dramatic readings, the late Maude Woodfork McElroy, an African American from Lebanon, is best known as being hired by the Quaker Oats Company to play the role of Aunt Jemima.

*Maude Woodfork, "Aunt Jemima".*

A newspaper story published in New York in 1947 reports that McElroy was chosen for the Aunt Jemima part from 80 applicants. The New York story goes on to say that the Lebanon native was to be paid "an annual salary running into five figures."

*William N. (Bill) Carter on Kennedy detail*

He was a member of President John Kennedy's Secret Service detail, a Washington attorney and insider for years, provided legal representation to the Rolling Stones on their first U.S. tour, and eventually took a path to Nashville that's allowed him to manage, represent, or promote some of the music industry's biggest names including Reba McEntire, Tanya Tucker, David Bowie, Lonestar, Waylon Jennings, Rodney Crowell, Carlene Carter, Shenandoah, TV/radio personality Ralph Emery, The Gaithers and several others. Outside the music business Bill Carter for many years also represented the Billy Graham Crusade and enjoyed a close relationship with Graham and the Graham family.

Following Kennedy's assassination Carter was enlisted by the Warren Commission to assist in its investigation and was assigned to interview Jack Ruby, the man who shot and killed Kennedy's assassin Lee Harvey Oswald.

*Bill Carter.*

Some of his high profile clients besides those previously listed have included Teamster boss Jimmy Hoffa and Federal Express founder Fred Smith. In 1980, Carter was credited with negotiating the return of Steve McQueen's body to the U.S. in just six hours after the actor's death in Juarez, Mexico.

In 2006, Carter published the book "Get Carter" about his life and career.

He and his wife Marlow live on Horn Springs Road in Lebanon.

*Dancing at the Opry*

A Lebanon businessman started something in 1952 that continued for decades to follow.

The late Ralph Sloan, who had an ownership interest in several Lebanon businesses, put his musical credits to work and began a square dance troupe that performed regularly on the Grand Ole Opry known as the Tennessee Travelers.

Ralph Sloan and the Tennessee Travelers danced on the Opry for 28 years until Sloan's death. His brother Melvin, who was a member of the original group, continued the tradition under the name the Melvin Sloan Dancers until 2002, at which time the Opry took over the group and renamed it the Grand Ole Opry Square Dancers under the leadership of Clyde Richardson.

Eddie Oliver, a Lebanon resident, began dancing with the Opry dancers under the tutelage of Ralph Sloan at the age of 13 and continued as a regular Opry performer for more than 50 years.

*DeFord Bailey, first African American to play the Opry*

A country music and blues star from the 1920s until 1941, DeFord Bailey, although from the Bellwood Community in rural east Wilson County, was seen frequently and often claimed by Lebanon.

He was the first African American performer to appear on the Grand Ole Opry in Nashville. A grandson of slaves, Bailey, who mastered several instruments, is best known for his talents with the harmonica. He learned to play the harmonica at the age of three, when he contracted polio. He was confined to bed for a year, during which time he began developing his distinctive style of playing.

Several records by Bailey were released in 1927 and 1928, all of them harmonica solos.

He appeared on WSM's Grand Ole Opry from 1927 to 1941 and was regarded as one of the show's most popular performers. During this period he toured with major country stars, including Uncle Dave Macon, Bill Monroe, and Roy Acuff. Like other black stars of his day traveling in the South and West, he faced difficulties in finding food and accommodations because of discriminatory Jim Crow laws.

*Allman Brothers attended Castle Heights*

In the late 1950s Duane and Greg Allman were junior school cadets at Castle Heights Military Academy in Lebanon and in 1969 formed the Allman Brothers Rock Band in Macon, GA.

Greg Allman, a gifted singer-songwriter, whom country-rock star Charlie Daniels once described as the "finest white blues singer" he'd ever heard, had an early life filled with tragedy that included the murder of his father when he was two years old and the death of his brother, Duane, in a motorcycle accident in 1971.

Duane was actually the brother credited with starting the band.

Gregg died at his home in Richmond Hill, GA in 2017, due to complications from liver cancer.

*Ben Hayslip chose a career in songwriting over athletics*

Living near Lebanon on a farm on Cairo Bend Road, Ben Hayslip has been one of Nashville's hottest songwriters since the late 2000s. He's been named ASCAP Songwriter of the Year twice, won some 20 ASCAP awards and been presented two Song of the Year Awards for "Honey Bee" and "It Goes Like This." In 2011, 2013 and 2014, Hayslip received the CMA Triple Play Award for having three number one songs in a 12-month period.

His career in music could have easily been sidestepped for a career as a professional athlete based on his record on the athletic field in high school and college.

In 1984, as a freshman, he was the starting quarterback on the Valdosta High School football team that won a state and national championship. In 1985 his family relocated to Evans, GA where he attended Evans High School near Augusta. He became an All-State first baseman and was instrumental in helping lead the Evans baseball team to a runner-up finish in the 1985 State Championship, and in his senior year his team won the State Championship with a 29-1 record and a number three national ranking by *USA Today*. After graduation, Hayslip attended Georgia Southern University where he was a member of the 1990 baseball team that participated in the College World Series in Omaha, NE. After graduating from Georgia Southern University in 1994 he moved to Nashville to pursue a career in country music.

Hayslip's songs have been recorded by Josh Turner, Martina McBride, Blake Shelton, Brooks and Dunn, and others.

*Lorrie Morgan charted first single in 1978*

Country music singer Lorrie Morgan lives in a private gated community just outside of Lebanon.

Morgan charted her first single in 1978, although she did not break into the top of the U.S. country charts until her 1989 single, "Trainwreck of Emotion." Since then, she has charted 40 songs on the Billboard Hot Country Singles & Tracks charts, with three number one hits.

*Bryan Wayne Galentine with a passion for life*

If you Google him, you'll find that his professional/stage name has been abbreviated to Bryan Wayne. He's written songs for some of country music's most familiar names including Big & Rich, Clay Walker, Rodney Carrington, Emerson Drive and others and, while this songwriter and performer who lives in Lebanon has a passion for music and the music industry, he's directed much of his energy since 2017 to another matter of great personal interest.

In 2017, Galentine was diagnosed with amyotrophic lateral sclerosis or ALS, a progressive and eventually terminal neurodegenerative disease that affects nerve cells in the brain and the spinal cord. Faced with the possibility of losing his ability to speak or sing, Galentine almost immediately embarked on a mission to create his own first ever album, "While You Wait." The album was released December 10, 2018.

Relating to others in 2018 about his battle with ALS, Galentine wrote,

"ALS has taught me to try my best, to not take a single second for granted. Some days it's easier said than done, but I'm trying.

"And it's taught me to better appreciate my wife, my sons, my family, my friends, and life in general. I wish I had gotten that wake-up call some other way, but if it took getting ALS to wake me up, so be it.

"I have decided instead of being angry and bitter about my diagnosis, I am going to take this opportunity to remind my friends and family how fleeting life is, and how important it is to appreciate every second."

*Johnny Carver took 'Tie a Yellow Ribbon' to number one*

The Lebanon resident gained fame in the mid-1970s with a number one country hit "Tie a Yellow Ribbon Round the Ole Oak Tree." For almost a decade from 1968 to 1977, Carver charted 15 Top 40 hits on the Billboard country charts.

He grew up in a rural area near Jackson, MS, and sang in a local country gospel quartet with his family. He formed his own band, the Capital Cowboys, and did a national tour in 1959, playing at clubs and fairs. He moved to Los Angeles in 1965, where he made regular appearances on local television and led a house band at the Palomino Club with such performers as Buck Owens, Johnny Cash, Patsy Cline, Linda Ronstadt, The Flying Burrito Brothers, Hoyt Axton, Willie Nelson, Merle Haggard, and Jerry Lee Lewis.

*Gretchen Wilson streaks to success with 'Redneck Woman'*

Gretchen Wilson, who has lived in Lebanon for several years in two different residences, both situated on large farms, debuted her talent and rose immediately to stardom in March 2004 with the Grammy Award-winning single "Redneck Woman," a number-one country hit.

Selling more than eight million records worldwide, Wilson has charted 13 singles on the Billboard country charts, of which five have gained Top Ten recognition.

# Chapter Five
# Weathering the Storms

Snow storms, ice accumulations, tornadoes, severe heat waves, flooding, and drought have all had their way with Lebanon since early settlers first located here more than 200 years ago.

On multiple occasions summer mercury readings have soared above the 100-degree mark.

Brief appearances of snow have been reported to have happened twice in June, once for about five minutes in 1923 and the second time for 15 minutes in 1930.

*Cadets at Castle Heights take time off from classes to enjoy sledding on "The Hill".*

The town's Square has been the site of a number of destructive flooding events. The Valentines Day flood in 1989 was responsible for taking the life of a person trapped in a car on South Cumberland Street about two blocks from the Square.

Tornadoes have ripped through residential subdivisions, hail has peppered cars and rooftops, and extended periods of drought have claimed millions of dollars in crop losses.

The Cumberland River has frozen over at least a couple times to the point that the packed ice floor was thick enough that cattle could be driven across the river near Hunters Point.

While there have been a number of significant weather happenings in and about Lebanon, perhaps there has been no greater weather occurrence here than the "Great Ice Storm of 1951."

This single weather event is remembered as the phenomenon that stopped Lebanon and Middle Tennessee for weeks.

Newspaper reports and history notes about the ice storm detail how the entire Middle Tennessee region was paralyzed for weeks.

*Lebanon merchant clears snow from store on the Square in 1972.*

The late Dr. Frank Burns, a former Wilson County historian, educator and newspaper editor, provided the following account about the 1951 ice storm.

"On January 28, rain turned to sleet in mid-afternoon.

"The next day the sleet froze to ice on streets and sidewalks.

"Then, there was freezing rain January 30 on the ice.

"On January 31, three inches of snow topped this off.

"On February 1, by 9 p.m., zero! Brilliant stars in a jet black sky.

"The world was frozen in glittering ice on every tree. At 6:45 a.m. on February 2, the thermometer read minus 12; at 8 a.m., 1 above.

"Finally, on February 3, the temperature, which was minus 6 at dawn, rose above freezing that afternoon. The worst was over. But the schools stayed closed for two weeks, and power lines all over the county were torn down from the weight of the ice on the wires and from falling trees. It took a month to get them all back up."

Many of Lebanon's most devastating weather events, resulting in substantial property damage, have been attributed to flooding and primarily flooding on the town Square from what's known as Town Creek.

One early historical note about Town Creek flooding dates back to 1865, as told in the "History of Wilson County."

Confederate troops, returning to Lebanon from the war, waded through existing water on May 25 while rain continued. At 3 a.m. the next morning the Public Square was submerged below as much as six feet of water. It's

*Heavy snowfall in 1965.*

said that a two-inch layer of mud and silt was deposited in every house and store in the immediate area of the Square.

On June 28, 1928, heavy rains caused Town Creek to flood to a height where men stood knee deep at the corner of West Main and Maple Street a block off the Square and waist deep in the Square's southwest corner.

What's been described as a torrential downpour falling in the late night of August 2, 1939 and continuing through the early morning hours caused the Town Creek to rush flood water to the Square with as much as four feet of water standing inside businesses on northwest side and a foot of water on the Square's east side.

A five-inch rain in 1949 caused Town Creek to flood the Square on June 15 and 16. The Creek overflowed first on the night of June 15, subsided and flooded the Square again the next day.

*Square under water believed to be a 1955 flood. In the photo is the old courthouse, Lebanon Bank and the H.G. Hills grocery store and on the opposite side of the Square, Seat's Studio.*

However, while these floods and others in later years were severe and caused great damage and loss of property, they pale in comparison to the floods of 1989 and 2010.

During the early morning hours of February 14, 1989, sirens atop the city's fire and police headquarters blared to warn local businessmen and nearby residents that the city's Square was in danger of flooding.

Flood waters were already slipping from the banks of Town Creek on

# Weathering the Storms

*Lebanon Square under water during 1989 flood.*

South Cumberland Street when the first warning signals sounded. A couple of hours passed. Water continued to move shoe sole deep from the creek's east side bank ever so slowly toward the Square.

Several merchants and others were casually drinking coffee and eating breakfast at the Ideal Cafe on the corner of Gay and South Cumberland and speculating if there was going to be a major flood or as had happened many times in the past just a gentle washing - not even curb high across the Square.

Another hour passed and now water was getting deeper and moving much closer to the Square. Businessmen began to scramble back to their stores around the Square. They placed sandbags at door fronts and put duct tape around windows and doors in a desperate attempt to seal openings because they knew now there was a major flood about to happen.

By 6 a.m. there were a half dozen or so boats on the Square - some with motors. Water was above parking meters in some places. Along store fronts on South Cumberland, a few hundred feet from the Square, the water had risen to above four feet.

Flood water raged through the Square and covered streets more than a block in any direction from the town's business center.

It was a disaster by any measurement. But worse than the hundreds of thousands of dollars in destroyed property was the loss of a single life.

A woman, according to police, ignored the warnings about the high water and attempted to drive her car through the rushing current. Her car stalled and became stranded on South Cumberland Street about a block and a half from the Square. Trying to escape she jumped from her car but was carried away by the flood water.

The Valentine Day flood of 1989 is remembered as the worst of the Town Creek floods for no other reason than the loss of life it claimed.

Following two days of torrential rains in 2010, the Town Creek flooded the Public Square again.

However, this time the event, deemed a 1,000-year flood by the National Weather Service, devastated much of Middle Tennessee.

It all began when a significant weather system brought heavy rain and severe thunderstorms beginning Saturday, May 1, continuing through Sunday, May 2, and finally ending on May 3. The Weather Bureau described the storm system as a stalled frontal boundary coupled with very moist air streaming northward from the Gulf and setting the stage for repeated rounds of heavy rainfall.

Lebanon's rainfall total for the period exceeded 13.5 inches. A one-day record amount, 7.24 inches, was set on May 2.

Not only did Town Creek leave its banks and flood the Lebanon Square but virtually all of Lebanon and Wilson County were affected. Roads were closed. Some were washed away. Homes and businesses alike suffered extensive damage.

There have been several other occasions when the Town Creek left its banks and brought flood water to the Square but these by far are the most memorable.

In what's told by the "History of Wilson County" to be the "worst storm of Wilson County's second century," four persons died, houses were destroyed and damage inside Lebanon's city limits was said to be more than $100,000.

On March 14, 1933, according to the history book, a "typical funnel cloud roared out of the open fields southwest of Lebanon at deep dusk - 8:14 p.m. - of a Tuesday evening."

The account of the event says that "within 60 seconds" much of the damage had been done. Cumberland University's Memorial Hall was damaged, windows broken, and the school's football field and stands demolished. The tornado continued on a swath east from Lebanon toward the Smith County line. It was on the route east of Lebanon near Bellwood where the four lives were claimed.

*Calendar of weather events*

The Calendar of Weather Events that have affected Lebanon has been compiled from a number of sources including the "History of Wilson County", the National Weather Service, The Lebanon Democrat, The Wilson Post, and the Old Farmer's Almanac Weather History publication.

It's noteworthy that official record keeping prior to 1900 was not always available as it is today and that certain weather events like tornados, hail storms and other occurrences have not been recorded as frequently as they have been in more recent years. Therefore, in the listing below, there may be some events that are omitted because there was no record of their occurrence or there may be certain inconsistencies because of conflicting reports.

Finally, the information provided in the calendar of weather events points to the local area experiencing more frequent and deeper snows and, in many cases, longer and colder winters prior to the late 1960s and mid-1970s than what has been recorded since, which some might argue is in agreement with global warming theories.

# Notes from Lebanon's First 200 Years

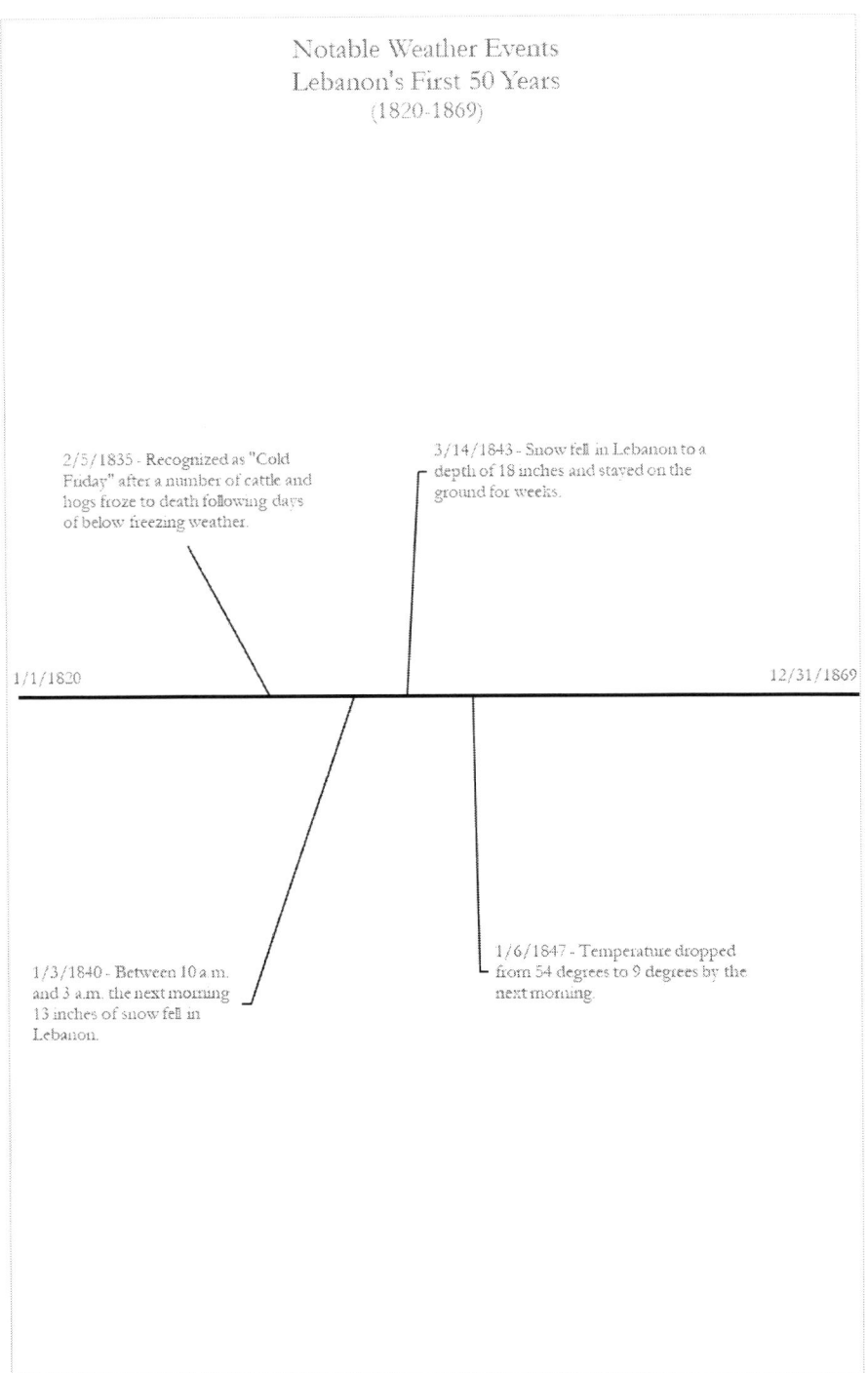

Notable Weather Events
Lebanon's First 50 Years
(1820-1869)

1/1/1820

12/31/1869

2/5/1835 - Recognized as "Cold Friday" after a number of cattle and hogs froze to death following days of below freezing weather.

3/14/1843 - Snow fell in Lebanon to a depth of 18 inches and stayed on the ground for weeks.

1/3/1840 - Between 10 a.m. and 3 a.m. the next morning 13 inches of snow fell in Lebanon.

1/6/1847 - Temperature dropped from 54 degrees to 9 degrees by the next morning.

# Weathering the Storms

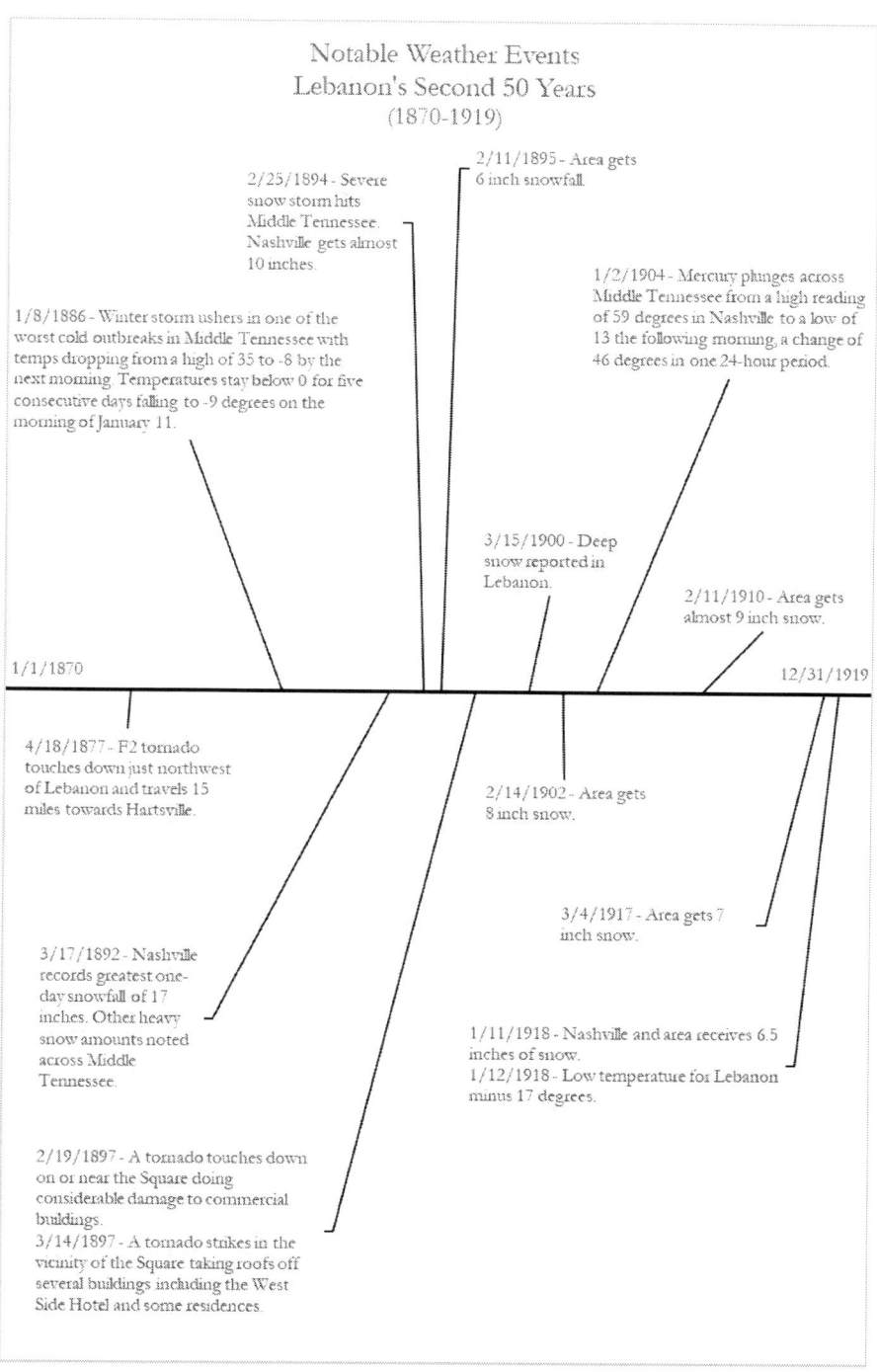

## Notable Weather Events
## Lebanon's Second 50 Years
## (1870-1919)

- 2/25/1894 - Severe snow storm hits Middle Tennessee. Nashville gets almost 10 inches.

- 2/11/1895 - Area gets 6 inch snowfall.

- 1/2/1904 - Mercury plunges across Middle Tennessee from a high reading of 59 degrees in Nashville to a low of 13 the following morning, a change of 46 degrees in one 24-hour period.

- 1/8/1886 - Winter storm ushers in one of the worst cold outbreaks in Middle Tennessee with temps dropping from a high of 35 to -8 by the next morning. Temperatures stay below 0 for five consecutive days falling to -9 degrees on the morning of January 11.

- 3/15/1900 - Deep snow reported in Lebanon.

- 2/11/1910 - Area gets almost 9 inch snow.

1/1/1870

12/31/1919

- 4/18/1877 - F2 tornado touches down just northwest of Lebanon and travels 15 miles towards Hartsville.

- 2/14/1902 - Area gets 8 inch snow.

- 3/4/1917 - Area gets 7 inch snow.

- 3/17/1892 - Nashville records greatest one-day snowfall of 17 inches. Other heavy snow amounts noted across Middle Tennessee.

- 1/11/1918 - Nashville and area receives 6.5 inches of snow.
- 1/12/1918 - Low temperature for Lebanon minus 17 degrees.

- 2/19/1897 - A tornado touches down on or near the Square doing considerable damage to commercial buildings.
- 3/14/1897 - A tornado strikes in the vicinity of the Square taking roofs off several buildings including the West Side Hotel and some residences.

# Notes from Lebanon's First 200 Years

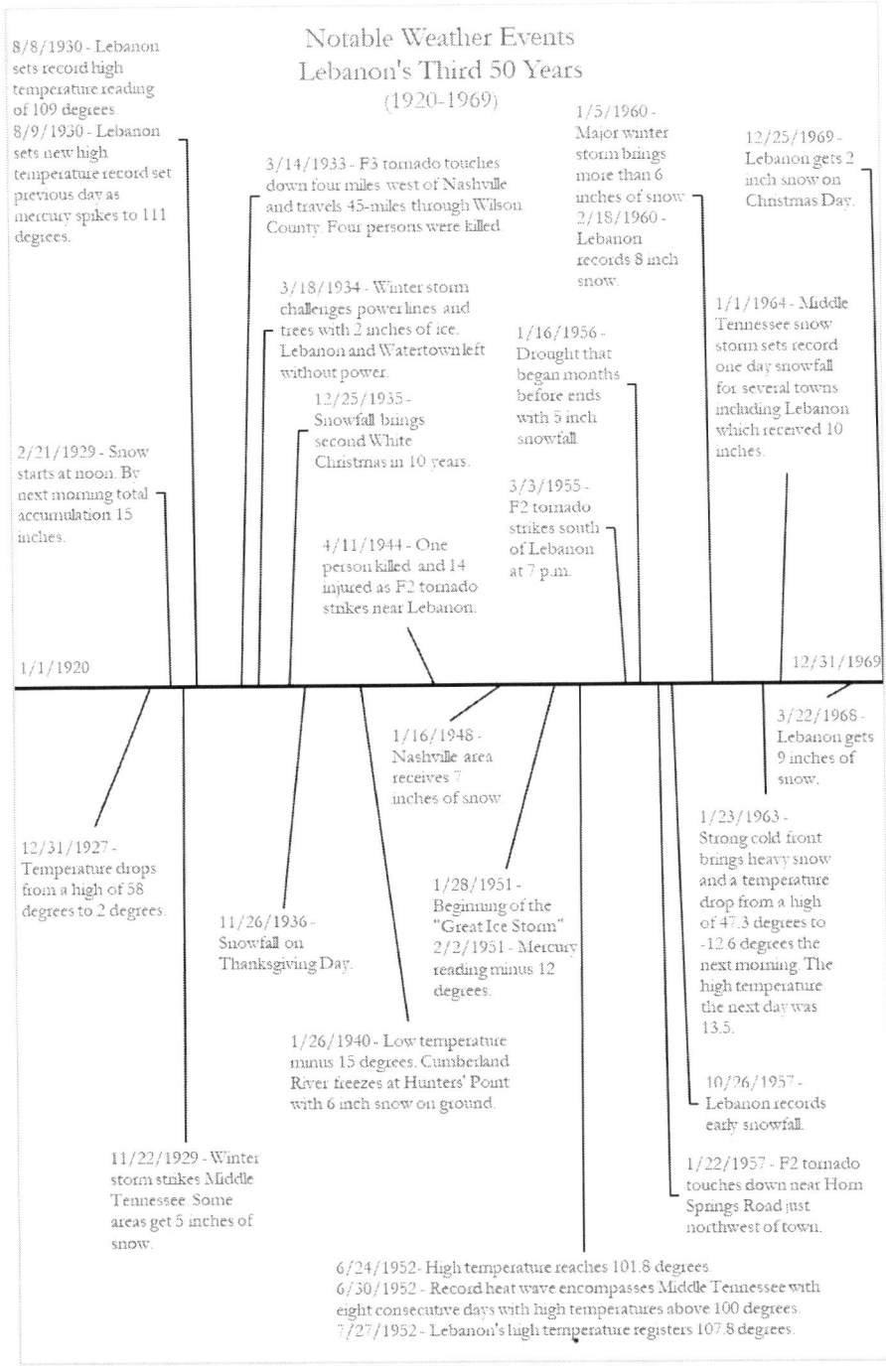

## Notable Weather Events
## Lebanon's Third 50 Years
## (1920-1969)

- 8/8/1930 - Lebanon sets record high temperature reading of 109 degrees
- 8/9/1930 - Lebanon sets new high temperature record set previous day as mercury spikes to 111 degrees.
- 2/21/1929 - Snow starts at noon. By next morning total accumulation 15 inches.
- 12/31/1927 - Temperature drops from a high of 58 degrees to 2 degrees.
- 11/22/1929 - Winter storm strikes Middle Tennessee. Some areas get 5 inches of snow.
- 3/14/1933 - F3 tornado touches down four miles west of Nashville and travels 45-miles through Wilson County. Four persons were killed.
- 3/18/1934 - Winter storm challenges power lines and trees with 2 inches of ice. Lebanon and Watertown left without power.
- 12/25/1935 - Snowfall brings second White Christmas in 10 years.
- 4/11/1944 - One person killed and 14 injured as F2 tornado strikes near Lebanon.
- 11/26/1936 - Snowfall on Thanksgiving Day.
- 1/16/1948 - Nashville area receives 7 inches of snow.
- 1/28/1951 - Beginning of the "Great Ice Storm"
- 2/2/1951 - Mercury reading minus 12 degrees.
- 1/26/1940 - Low temperature minus 15 degrees. Cumberland River freezes at Hunters' Point with 6 inch snow on ground.
- 6/24/1952 - High temperature reaches 101.8 degrees.
- 6/30/1952 - Record heat wave encompasses Middle Tennessee with eight consecutive days with high temperatures above 100 degrees.
- 7/27/1952 - Lebanon's high temperature registers 107.8 degrees.
- 1/16/1956 - Drought that began months before ends with 5 inch snowfall.
- 3/3/1955 - F2 tornado strikes south of Lebanon at 7 p.m.
- 1/5/1960 - Major winter storm brings more than 6 inches of snow.
- 2/18/1960 - Lebanon records 8 inch snow.
- 12/25/1969 - Lebanon gets 2 inch snow on Christmas Day.
- 1/1/1964 - Middle Tennessee snow storm sets record one day snowfall for several towns including Lebanon which received 10 inches.
- 3/22/1968 - Lebanon gets 9 inches of snow.
- 1/23/1963 - Strong cold front brings heavy snow and a temperature drop from a high of 47.3 degrees to -12.6 degrees the next morning. The high temperature the next day was 13.5.
- 10/26/1957 - Lebanon records early snowfall.
- 1/22/1957 - F2 tornado touches down near Horn Springs Road just northwest of town.

1/1/1920 — 12/31/1969

# Weathering the Storms

## Notable Weather Events
## Lebanon's Past 50 Years
## (1970-2019)

**3/25/1982** - Area between Baddour Parkway and Coles Ferry Pike experiences hail storm at 12:35 p.m. with 1.75 inch hail.

**1/15/1978** - High temperature reaches 27 degrees. Mercury does not rise above freezing for seven consecutive days.

**2/17/1976** - Tornado cuts 15.2 mile path south of I-40 traveling northeast to South Cumberland Street.

**3/19/1996** - Area receives 8 inch snow.

**1/6/1996** - Winter storm bring freezing rain that changes to sleet in the afternoon and then to all snow by evening.

**2/14/1989** - Major flooding on Square. One death recorded.

**4/27/1992** - Tornado hits near Lebanon at intersection of I-40 and I-840.

**11/30/2004** - Flash flooding occurs at 2:20 p.m. Square closed because of high water.

**5/10/2004** - Hail reported north of town center. Hail size .88 of an inch.

**7/9/2003** - Hail storm at 4:29 p.m. with 1 inch hail just north of Square.

**5/1/2007** - Severe drought begins and continues through November of 2008. All counties in Tennessee designated disaster areas. Area farmers suffer millions of dollars in crop damage. Wilson County Fair reports attendance down more than 12 percent (366,641 attend Fair) because of severe heat wave.

**12/1/2008** - Drought that began in May 2007 ends thanks to rains in November.

**8/4/2010** - Afternoon temperature soars to 100 degrees with heat index of 110 degrees to 104 degrees.

**3/2/2012** - At 4:34 p.m. 2 inch size hail reported in several areas of town.

**1/1/1970** ——————————————————————— **12/31/2019**

**4/27/1971** - F3 rated tornado hits south of Lebanon at 8 p.m. injuring three followed by hail storm with 1.75 inch hail.

**1/21/1985** - Lebanon temperature drops to -20 degrees, a record low.

**7/9/1988** - Lebanon's high temperature hits 105...

**1/16/2003** - Snow starts falling by 9 a.m. or so by midday several inches are on the ground. When snow ends some areas have as much as 7 inches.

**8/15/2007** - Excessive heat blamed for death of 48-year-old Fair worker from New Jersey here to help set-up Fair rides. Temperature reaches 104 degrees.

**1/29/2010** - Winter storm brings 4 inch snow.

**2/16/2015** - Ice, sleet and freezing rain mixed with snow downs power lines.

**9/14/1979** - One day rainfall record set in Lebanon at 6.51 inches. (Record broken on May 3, 2010 when 7.24 inches of rain fell.)

**6/4/1985** - F2 tornado touches down about two miles west of Public Square at 4:30 p.m. Tornado traveled six mile corridor from Northern Road off Hwy. 109 to west Lebanon crossing into South Fork and Shenandoah subdivisions. Hail storm followed with 2.5 inch hail.

**5/1/2010** - Torrential rains begin as a weather front stalls over much of Middle Tennessee. For Lebanon the first 24-hour period brings more than 6 inches of rain.

**5/2/2010** - Historic rain event in Middle Tennessee continues to bring record rainfall and floods much of Wilson County. Rain total for...

**4/22/2017** - Flash flood at 1:30 requires person to be rescued on South Cumberland Street from flood waters.

53

# Chapter Six
# Lebanon Puts Folks in Powerful Places

For more than two centuries Lebanon has produced a number of national, state, and local leaders who have made monumental contributions at every level of government.

Cumberland University gets much of the credit for the lengthy list of notable leaders as it has been an incubator of sorts for producing civic minded public servants who have given of their time and resources to be members of the U.S. Congress, the judiciary, state and local elected officials, and who have served in other capacities to include the ministry and military.

*Cumberland's list of distinguished graduates*

Atop the list of Cumberland's most prestigious graduates is the late Cordell Hull, who served as U.S. Secretary of State during World War II. Prior to being named Secretary of State, Hull served in the Tennessee House of Representatives, the U.S. Congress and U.S. Senate. Generally recognized as the "father" of the United Nations, Hull served as Secretary of State for 11 years, the longest term anyone has ever held the post.

Cumberland's list of distinguished alumni includes some 50 college and university presidents, 66 U.S. Congressmen, 11 state governors, scores of state and federal judges, two U.S. ambassadors, and two Justices of the U.S. Supreme Court. The alumni rolls also include hundreds who have held state and locally elected offices.

*Five Tennessee governors lived here*

Five of Tennessee's governors have claimed Lebanon as their home at one time or another including Sam Houston, elected in 1827; James

*Hundreds gather on the Lebanon Square to hear Buford Ellington's campaign speech in his race for governor.*

Chamberlain "Lean Jimmy" Jones, elected in 1840; William Bowen Campbell, elected in 1850; James D. Porter, elected in 1874; and Frank G. Clement, elected in 1952, 1954, and 1962. Both Porter and Clement lived in Lebanon, while attending Cumberland University. Robert L. Carothers was elected governor in 1863 but was not permitted to assume the office because the state was under occupation by federal troops.

Largely to Cumberland's credit, Lebanon in past years has been a recognized breeding ground for some of the state's and nation's most powerful leaders.

*He started a movement that continues today on national stage*

Having as much influence on American politics as any single elected official was arguably an African American man who studied and lived for a short while in Lebanon and became one of the principal founders of the National Association for the Advancement of Colored People, the NAACP.

William Edward Burghardt (W.E.B.) Du Bois, an American sociologist, historian, civil rights activist, author, and writer, who grew up in Great Barrington, Massachusetts, came to Lebanon in 1886 at age 18 to attend a teachers' institute and to earn his teacher certification, a requirement for him to teach school. At the time he was enrolled at Fisk University in Nashville.

Being from an area originally where there was little racial bigotry or conflict between whites and blacks, Du Bois' travels in the South provided a new experience for him that exposed him for the first time to heightened racism, Jim Crow laws, suppression of black voting, and lynchings.

After receiving a bachelor's degree from Fisk, Du Bois attended Harvard College. Harvard at the time did not accept course credits from Fisk and Du Bois paid his way through three years at Harvard with money from summer jobs, an inheritance, scholarships, and loans from friends in order to be awarded a Harvard bachelor's degree in 1890. In 1891, he received a scholarship to attend the sociology graduate school at Harvard.

In 1892, Du Bois received a fellowship from the John F. Slater Fund for the Education of Freedmen to attend the University of Berlin for graduate work. After returning from Europe, Du Bois completed his graduate studies and in 1895 he was the first African American to earn a Ph.D. from Harvard University.

Du Bois' writings and his reflections on the early years he spent in the South, a portion of that time here in Lebanon and as a school teacher to children of former slaves at a one room school in nearby Alexandria in neighboring DeKalb County, became the foundation for a movement that has served to change the political and cultural scene in the U.S. forever.

*William D. (Bill) Baird ignites progress*

In more recent years the late William D. (Bill) Baird, who served as Lebanon mayor in the mid-1950s, has gotten much of the recognition for moving the town forward with a progressive plan to attract industry. It was Baird, who created a first-of-its-kind industrial park in Tennessee in Lebanon, and who also was instrumental in authoring state legislation

*The old Lebanon Courthouse stands on what is now a parking lot on the town's Public Square.*

making it possible for cities like Lebanon to offer industrial bonds to attract industry. After his time as mayor, Baird served as a state senator and Tennessee's Lieutenant Governor.

Because of Baird and other high profile elected officials from here who were serving in state offices, Lebanon was viewed for some 40 years as a bastion of power in state government.

*At the time of this photo Don Simpson (standing behind the counter) was the County Court Clerk for Wilson County. He later was elected County Executive. The photo was taken at the old Courthouse on the Lebanon Square.*

# Lebanon Puts Folks in Powerful Places

*Four decades of political power*

During this four decade period stretching into the 1990s **Frank Clement**, who had gone to school at Cumberland, served as governor; **Baird** served in the state senate and became lieutenant governor; the late **Ramon T. Davis**, a Lebanon insurance agency owner, served a term as state treasurer; the late **Gwendolyn Davis** (wife of Ramon Davis) served in the cabinets of **Gov. Buford Ellington** and **Gov. Winfield Dunn**; Lebanon farmer and businessman **Johnny Trice** had been a key figure in Gov. Buford Ellington's election and also directed a number of local candidates' races; **State Rep. Gentry Crowell** was elected Tennessee Secretary of State; Lebanon attorney **Bob Rochelle** was elected to the state senate and rose to the ranking position of Speaker Pro-tempore; **Carl Wallace**, who had been editor of The Lebanon Democrat, was appointed The State Adjutant General by **Gov. Ray Blanton** and placed in charge

*Planning a political campaign in Wilson County for Gov. Buford Ellington are Johnny Trice, Gentry Crowell and Jerry McFarland.*

of the state's military department; Lebanon businessman **Charles Bell** was appointed Commissioner of General Services by Gov. Blanton; Lebanon attorney **Comer Donnell** was director of Petroleum Taxes for the Tennessee Department of Revenue and in 1989 appointed Public Defender for the 15th Judicial District; Castle Heights graduate **Tommy Thompson**, from Hartsville, was appointed District Attorney for 15th Judicial District by Gov. Blanton; farmer and county commissioner **Jerry McFarland** was named the state's emergency services director; and **Bob Clement** who had been president of Cumberland University and is the son of Gov. Clement, was elected to the U.S. Congress representing Nashville. And also during this period the late **George Harding** was a power broker of sorts as he was a member of the Wilson County Commission, county road superintendent at one point, and behind the scenes ran a number of political campaigns including election campaigns for Sen. Baird.

Keep in mind, while there were other politically powerful personalities in Wilson County, this list is restricted to only those in Lebanon.

The list should probably also include Lebanon mayors **Charles Loyd**, who served a stint in Washington with the Federal Trade Commission and **Willis H. (Tex) Maddox**, who also served as a state representative as did Mayor **Jack Lowery**.

*Favorite son becomes Memphis mayor*

One of Lebanon's favorite sons, A C Wharton, Jr., left home in the 1960s, earned an undergraduate degree in Political Science at Tennessee State University and a law degree from the University of Mississippi.

Wharton, the son of an African American sharecropper, who ensured that each of his five children received a college degree, held a faculty post at the Ole Miss law school for several years and in 1980 began his climb in politics when he was appointed as Chief Public Defender for Shelby County, Tennessee.

Lebanon Puts Folks in Powerful Places

In 2002, he was elected the first African American mayor of Shelby County. He was reelected county mayor in 2006 and in 2009 Wharton was elected mayor of the City of Memphis in a special election receiving about 60 percent of the votes cast among the field of 25 candidates seeking the office. He remained mayor of Memphis until December 31, 2015, after losing a reelection bid in October.

He and his wife, Ruby, also an attorney, continue to live in Memphis. The couple has three adult sons.

*Lebanon mayor played role in conviction of Gov. Blanton*

Jack Lowery, a prominent criminal defense attorney, who served as Lebanon's mayor for one term from 1974 to 1978, was a primary force in helping authorities crack a case in which a Tennessee governor and some of his cronies were selling pardons and paroles near the end of the governor's term in office.

In 1976, a man who identified himself as Bob Roundtree came to Lowery's office on the Square in Lebanon knowing Lowery was trying to get a client in state prison for vehicular homicide released through an executive clemency proceeding. Roundtree told Lowery he could assist him on his client's clemency request; that he could tell him when his client would be released; and that there would be no conditions on him being freed from state prison. However, there would be a price to be paid for the release, $20,000. Following Roundtree's visit, Lowery put on paper notes from his conversation and turned the matter over to investigators. The FBI gained access to Lowery's report which contributed significantly to the agency's investigation of Gov. Ray Blanton's administration and the arrest and conviction of several of the governor's aides.

In 1979, near the end of his term, Blanton issued pardons to 52 state prisoners, including 20 convicted murderers. As Blanton signed one of the pardons, he stated, "this takes guts."

Lebanon's Gentry Crowell, who was Secretary of State at the time, had become disgusted with Blanton and his pardons and replied, "some people have more guts than brains."

Learning that Blanton was planning to announce more pardons and looking for a way to stop him, state leaders, meeting in secret, found that the state constitution was vague as it addressed when a newly elected governor must be sworn into office. Taking advantage of what they had learned, the leadership decided to swear in Lamar Alexander, who had won the 1978 gubernatorial election, three days before the traditional inauguration day.

Although never formally charged in the pardons matter, Blanton was eventually indicted on charges of mail fraud, conspiracy, and extortion for selling liquor licenses. He was convicted and sentenced to federal prison. Released on July 18, 1986 after serving 22 months, he returned to Tennessee.

*First black, first woman elected to City Council*

In 1985, voters in Lebanon went to the polls and made history as they elected the first African American to serve on the Lebanon City Council and the first female.

Fred Burton, who serves on the council currently, was the first black to be elected to the post and Jeannie Smith in the same election became the first woman to serve on the council.

*Tobacco chewing lawyer puts fire in race*

In 1970, Tennessee found itself knee deep in a hotly contested U.S. Senate race that became even more inflamed when a tobacco chewing country lawyer in Lebanon abandoned his own political party in support of the Republican candidate.

Sen. Albert Gore, Sr., a three term Democrat, was being challenged by a well-financed and popular Republican Congressman, Bill Brock, whose family had made its fortune in the candy business with a

Chattanooga company bearing their same name.

The early favorite in the campaign was Sen. Gore, whose son, Al, some 23 years later would be elected Vice President on a ticket with Bill Clinton.

But Gore's lead began to fade as Brock's campaign hit the airwaves charging that the veteran Tennessee senator had forgotten about the folk at home while getting comfortable in the ways of the Potomac for the past 18 years.

Fuel was added to the campaign fire when Lebanon attorney Alfred MacFarland, a longtime prominent Democrat,

*Celebrating the opening of Lebanon's new post office are from left Post Master Addison Barry, U.S. Rep. Joe Evins, person not identified, Mayor Charles Loyd and U.S. Sen. Albert Gore, Sr.*

split ranks with his own party and headed a group called "Democrats for Bill Brock."

MacFarland's contribution and his statewide role with the Brock campaign was viewed as being instrumental in helping to lead Democrats to the opposite side of the ballot and casting their votes for Gore's Republican foe.

Winning the election, Brock and national Republicans wanted to repay MacFarland for his support.

MacFarland was nominated to serve on the federal government's Interstate Commerce Commission. His seat on the ICC was one held by a Democrat. His appointment by President Richard Nixon to the commission was challenged by Democrats who argued that because of his role in the Brock election campaign he couldn't be considered a Democrat.

*A young first term Congressman Albert Gore, Jr., speaks to the Lebanon Lions Club.*

MacFarland was eventually confirmed by the Senate, served out his term on the ICC, and returned to his law practice on West Market Street in Lebanon.

MacFarland's role in Brock's campaign and his nomination to the ICC caught the eye of the national press who dubbed him as a "tobacco chewing country lawyer from Lebanon, Tennessee."

This same year a little known dentist from Memphis beat another Democrat in the state's gubernatorial race.

Winfield Dunn, became the first Republican governor to occupy the state Capitol since reconstruction. He defeated Democrat John Jay Hooker, whose family roots are based in Lebanon.

*Cumberland places two on U.S. Supreme Court*
Justice Howell Edmunds Jackson

Howell Edmunds Jackson, a Cumberland Law School graduate, was nominated to the U.S. Supreme Court in 1893 by President Benjamin Harrison. His career also included a term as a U.S. Senator representing Tennessee and a judgeship on the U.S. Court of Appeals for the Sixth Circuit. Jackson lived only 63 years, dying in 1895.

Justice Horace H. Lurton

When Horace H. Lurton was appointed to the U.S. Supreme Court in 1909 at age 66, he became the oldest nominee ever to the high court. Born in Newport, Kentucky and raised in Clarksville, he attended the University of Chicago in 1860 but joined the Confederate Army at the outbreak of the Civil War. Twice during the war he was captured by Union forces. Lurton was a graduate of the Cumberland Law School.

*Local contributions to state supreme court*
## Justice Allison B. Humphreys

Judge Humphreys had a brilliant career as a member of the judiciary. He was appointed to the Tennessee Supreme Court by Gov. Buford Ellington in 1967 and was elected to a full term on the court in 1968. Judge Humphreys retired from the supreme court in 1974.

Born June 28, 1906, in Lebanon, he was a graduate of Castle Heights Military Academy and held an undergraduate degree and law degree from Cumberland University.

He began the practice of law in Lebanon in 1929, served as assistant district attorney general, Fifth Judicial Circuit from 1937 to 1940; circuit judge, Fifth Judicial Circuit, from 1941 to 1942; acting dean and professor of law, Cumberland University Law School, 1942 to 1945; assistant to attorney general and reporter, 1943 to 1952; state solicitor general, 1952 to 1960; appointed to the Tennessee Court of Appeals in 1960 prior to joining the state Supreme Court.

## Justice Robert Looney Caruthers

Robert Looney Caruthers, a professor of law at Cumberland University, was appointed to the state supreme court in 1852. He was one of three judges elected in the first popular election of the court in 1854. He served until resigning in 1861. Born in Smith County, he was clerk of Tennessee House of Representatives, 1823; attorney general for his district, 1827-1832; brigadier general, Tennessee Militia, 1834; and Wilson County representative in state legislature, 1853. He and A. O. P. Nicholson are credited with compiling the Statutes of Tennessee in 1836.

Carothers served as a member of Congress, 1841-43; delegate to Peace Conference at Washington, 1861; member of Provisional Congress of Confederacy; elected governor of Tennessee, 1863, but never took office because of War between the States.

### Justice Chester C. Chattin

Chester C. Chattin was a 1930 graduate of the Cumberland Law School and was appointed to the state supreme court by Gov. Frank G. Clement in 1965. He was elected to a full term on the court in 1966.

### Justice Grafton Green

Grafton Green, born in Lebanon, was elected in 1910, 1918, 1926, 1934, and 1942 to the state supreme court and was chief justice from 1923 to 1947.

### Justice Nathan Green

Nathan Green, a professor of Law at Cumberland, was elected in 1831 and defeated John Catron in 1835 to be judge of the new supreme court under the Constitution of 1834. He retired from the court in 1852.

### Justice Horace H. Harrison

Horace H. Harrison, born in Lebanon, was a justice of the state supreme court member in 1868. He was principal clerk of the state senate, 1851-52; U.S. district attorney for Middle Tennessee, 1863-66, 1872; chancellor, Nashville District, 1867, to 1868; member of Congress, 1873-75; vice president of Republican National Convention, 1876; and member of the state legislature, 1880-81.

### Justice Joe W. Henry

Joe W. Henry, a graduate of the Cumberland University Law School, was elected to the state supreme court on August 1, 1974. He became chief justice of the court in 1979 and served in that role until his death in June 1980. He was a state representative for one term, 1948-50, and served as The State Adjutant General from 1953 to 1959.

### Justice Horace H. Lurton

Horace H. Lurton, a graduate of the Cumberland Law School, was elected to the state supreme court in 1886; elected chief justice in 1893; and resigned in 1893 to accept appointment as U.S. circuit judge of Sixth Circuit. He was appointed justice of U.S. Supreme Court in 1909 and served until his death in 1914.

### Justice A. B. Neil

A. B. Neil was appointed to the state supreme court in 1942. A former dean and professor of the Cumberland Law School, Neil was elected to the supreme court in 1942, 1950 and 1958 and elected chief justice in 1947.

### Justice Charles O'Brien

Charles O'Brien, a Cumberland Law graduate, was appointed to the state supreme court in 1987 by Gov. Ned McWherter; elected to the remainder of an unexpired term in 1988; reelected in 1990 for an eight-year term; and retired 1994.

### Justice Weldon B. White

Weldon B. White, a Cumberland professor of Law, was appointed to the state supreme court in 1961.

# Notes from Lebanon's First 200 Years

*Those who have served the City of Lebanon*

The following list includes mayors and chief administrators of the City of Lebanon. Terms of office and titles vary. Many of the early officials were in office for only one year.

1808 - 19 John Allcorn, chairman
1820 - 22 Edmund Crutcher, mayor
1823 - David Marshall
1824 - 25 Joseph Johnson
1826 - John S. Topp
1827 - Harry L. Douglas
1828 - Issac Golladay
1829 - 30 John Muirhead
1831 - George H. Bullard
1832 - E. A. White
1833 - Michael Yeager
1834 - John Hearn
1835 - George H. Bullard
1836 - Joseph Johnson
1837 - E. G. Cain
1838 - George F. McWhirter
1839 - John Hearn
1840 - 41 George F. McWhirter
1842 - A. W. Vick (resigned)
       Thomson Anderson (resigned)
       George F. McWhirter
1843 - 57 Josiah S. McClain
1865 - Lawrence Sypert
1866 - 69 R. E. Thompson
1873 - Sam G. Stratton
1876 - R. E. Thompson
1878 - 80 E. E. Beard
1880 - 82 A. B. Fonville
1882 - 86 J. Matt Woodard (President of Taxing District)
1886 - 90 Sam Golladay
1890 - 93 J. Neal MacKenzie
1893 - 98 B. W. Cox
1898 - 1900 J. W. Huddleston
1900 - 02 H. L. Coe
1902 - 07 Alex M. McClain
1907 - 08 H. L. Coe
1908 - 10 B. J. Dillard
1910 - 12 E. E. Beard (Chm. City Commission)
1912 - Alex McGlothlin
1912 - 19 Andrew B. Martin
1919 - 21 F. C. Stratton
1921 - Will A. Hale
1921 - 23 O. B. Cleveland
1923 - 24 T. E. Ellis
1924 - 25 F. C. Stratton
1925 - 30 A. A. Adams
1930 - 48 Frank Buchanan
1948 - 58 William D. Baird
1958 - 70 Charles D. Loyd
1970 - 74 Willis H. (Tex) Maddox
1974 - 78 Jack Lowery
1978 - 90 Willis H. (Tex) Maddox
1990 - 94 Bobby Jewell
1994 - 08 Don Fox
2008 - 16 Philip Craighead
2016 - Bernie Ash

# Chapter Seven
# Getting Here from There

Transportation gets an abundance of kudos when local officials speak about Lebanon's growth and vibrant economy.

In the 1960s Lebanon became connected with the rest of the world so-to-speak when the interstate highway system running east and west, I-40, was completed between some cities and nearing completion between others.

Opportunity was even expanded for Lebanon as other interstate routes were put in service.

*Taking their carriage to the Weir house on South College Street in 1894 are (front) Mrs. Bessie Weir Doak and Mr. Alice Williamson Hooker and in the rear seat Miss Amy Weir and Miss Martha Martin Burke.*

*West Main Street is still a dirt road in the late 1890s. The home on the left, now Ligon and Bobo Funeral Home, was built in 1828 by Robert L. Caruthers, a former Congressman, Tennessee governor, and state Supreme Court Justice. Winstead Paine Bone, in his book, A History of Cumberland University, wrote that Caruthers, "had more to do with the founding of Cumberland University than any other person." He was appointed president of the school's first board of trustees in 1842, and helped the school secure a charter in December of the following year. He remained president of the board until his death in 1882.*

One good example of the importance of the interstate highway system to Lebanon, as it relates to connectivity to the rest of the nation, is the fact that neighboring Nashville is one of only four U.S. cities where six interstate legs converge within the city's boundaries: I-65 North and South, I-40 East and West, and I-24 East and West.

This advantage coupled with connections provided by I-840 places Lebanon in a unique position to be within a day's drive of 75 percent of the nation's population east of the Mississippi River.

Before the interstates, Lebanon relied on U.S. Hwy. 70, a mostly two

Getting Here from There

*A boat pushes goods on the Cumberland River in 1890.*

lane highway running east and west, and U.S. Hwy. 231, a route running north and south, also a two lane road. While these highways were effective and valuable to Lebanon and Wilson County at a time when traffic did not crowd highways so much, they began to be problems when more motorists, including commercial truckers, took to the road.

Much credit is given to I-40 and I-840 for Lebanon's job growth in recent years as the two highways have made the community logistically attractive for a number of new industries and businesses including major trucking companies that have established important shipping hubs here.

*Changing gas price sign during a gas war in the 1960s.*

71

Notes from Lebanon's First 200 Years

*Watertown/Sparta Pike I-40 clover leaf freshly opened in 1965.*

*Access to air travel*

Another major advantage Lebanon enjoys with respect to transportation is its accessibility to air travel.

Nashville's International Airport is less than 30 minutes from virtually any address inside Lebanon's city limits, and from the city's west side the travel time is even less.

But beyond the recognized amenity of an international airport being nearby, Lebanon also maintains a very capable local airport with a 5,000 foot runway that accommodates and services a wide variety of commercial and private air traffic.

On April 30, 1919 the first airplane known to land in Wilson County landed in Lebanon at what at the time was known as the Fairgrounds. The plane was an Army aircraft flown from Murfreesboro to Lebanon to promote the Liberty Loan Drive, a bond drive to help cover the U.S. government's expenses for World War I.

In 1933, a group of interested citizens filed an application to the Civil Works Administration for funds to build an airport on about 45-acres of land near Franklin Road at what is essentially the same location where the Lebanon airport is today. The grant was approved and work began on a

2,500-foot airstrip built entirely by hand with an army of workers using picks and shovels.

Cumberland University acquired the airport in 1939 for $5,000 and used the facility to conduct pilot training until a time shortly after the U.S. entered World War II. Cumberland's connection to the airport and the airport's closeness to the university's campus where housing was available are said to be two major reasons that contributed to Cumberland being selected as the site for the Second Army's headquarters during the World War II maneuvers here.

The Nashville Flying service bought the airport from Cumberland in 1943 for the same $5,000 price Cumberland had paid four years earlier. By this time the airport property contained 75 acres.

The airport was sold again three years later and eventually purchased by the City of Lebanon in 1953 for $10,000.

Since this time a number of improvements have been made to the airport as city and county leaders came to realize it is an important factor in attracting new industry and commercial development to the local area.

In May 2017, a new two-story terminal building was opened along with a new road entrance to the airport. Besides providing corporate conference rooms, a pilots' lounge, public waiting area, and quiet room, the new terminal is also the host site for offices of the Wilson County Joint Economic and Community Development Board and the Lebanon Airport Commission.

Today's Lebanon Municipal Airport occupies an area of 256 acres and maintains two runways including a 5,000-foot asphalt airstrip and an 1,801-foot turf runway.

Several terminals are located on the property housing corporate jet aircraft as well as privately owned single and twin-engine planes.

In recent years much of the advancement and improvements provided for the Lebanon airport came as a result of the efforts of two longtime members of the Airport Commission, T.O. Cragwall, a former member of the Lebanon City Council, and John Baugh, an extraordinary aviation enthusiast, who served on the boards of the Experimental Aircraft Association and Tennessee Aeronautics Commission and who was inducted into the Tennessee Aviation Hall of Fame in 2004. Baugh's wife, Debra, was inducted into the Tennessee Aviation Hall of Fame in 2019.

*Getting here by rail*

"If they're not hauling it, they're not making it," is a phrase often quoted by Anthony Linn, a former director of the Nashville and Eastern Railroad, when discussing the health and well-being of the U.S. economy and his always verbose enthusiasm for railroads and the important role they play in moving freight.

A railroad has been bringing goods to Lebanon and shipping product

*Steam engine train bringing in freight in 1890.*

out since the late 1800s. Local milling operations like Barry Carter (later Martha White Flour) and businesses like Fakes and Hooker Lumber Company that were established in Lebanon during this era relied on rail service.

In 1869, the first spike was driven about a half mile south of Lebanon's Square to begin construction of a 30-mile stretch of track. This would mark the beginning of rail's history in Lebanon that has seen multiple owners, shutdowns and start-ups over a period approaching 150 years.

Early operators of the local railroad included the Tennessee and Pacific; Nashville, Chattanooga and St. Louis; Nashville and Knoxville; and the Tennessee Central.

Struggling financially for several years, the Tennessee Central abandoned its track in May 1968. Several larger railway companies took over some of the more lucrative segments of the Tennessee Central line but many communities were left with no rail service and Lebanon, as it turned out, would be one of those.

Lebanon regained rail service in 1986, when track abandoned by the Tennessee Central was reclaimed by the Nashville and Eastern Rail Authority, a quasi-government entity authorized by state government. The rail authority, which included members from Wilson, Davidson, Smith and Putnam counties, entered into a long-term lease agreement with the Nashville and Eastern Railroad Company to provide freight rail service to communities along the 137 miles of track extending from Nashville to Monterey east of Cookeville.

Since the new rail service was initiated, a number of new companies creating hundreds of new jobs have been recruited to Lebanon and located near the rail line so that they can take advantage of rail service.

The Nashville and Eastern Railroad is also the home of the Music City Star commuter rail service which runs between Nashville and Lebanon. The Music City Star, operated by the Regional Transportation Authority, began commuter service in 2006. It remains the only commuter rail line in Tennessee. The most recent report on annual ridership numbers for the Music City Star, the 2018 fiscal year, shows that were nearly 300,000 passenger trips for the 12-month period. The commuter train's first full year of operation saw just more than 100,000 passenger trips.

The Nashville and Eastern Railroad was sold in January 2019 to the R.J. Corman Railroad Group.

*Music City Star*

# Chapter Eight
## The Learning Process, Schools

Those who left Lebanon for careers and positions of prominence in other parts of the world and those who chose to remain in Lebanon as community leaders, merchants, farmers, and industrial employees all have one thing in common.

The roots of their education, for whatever their goals and purpose in life, emerged from classrooms and teachers here.

A U.S. Secretary of State, Cordell Hull, was educated in the law here. W.E.B. Du Bois, a founder of the NAACP and the first African American to be awarded a doctorate degree from Harvard, came to Lebanon one summer to earn a teacher's certificate. The co-founders of Cracker Barrel, the late Dan Evins and Tommy Lowe, are products of Lebanon schools. And there are hundreds of others who received their education in Lebanon and have gone forth to become distinguished military leaders, U.S. Congressmen, governors, entrepreneurs, and business leaders.

Local schools made an everlasting impression on these lives just as they have on thousands of others.

In the early to mid-1800s schools in Lebanon and Wilson County were private schools.

The first high school in Lebanon was Campbell Academy. It moved to a site in Lebanon in 1828 near where the Wilson County Justice Center is today which formerly was the structure in which the old Lebanon High School and later the Lebanon Junior High and Highland Heights schools were located on North Cumberland Street. Campbell Academy, founded in 1806, was originally located about eight miles west of Lebanon on Hickory Ridge Road. In 1854 Campbell was merged with Cumberland

University Preparatory School.

Another private school, Abbe Institute, a school for female students only, was started in the 1830s by Harriet Abbe and her sister Ann Kilborn of Connecticut. Their school was located across from Campbell Academy.

Through the mid and late 1800s several other private schools were opened in Lebanon including a female seminary on the south side of East Main Street by the Baptist Church in 1859; the Corona Female Institute in 1866 on West Main Street; and the Maple Hill Seminary in 1880 about three miles west of Lebanon on what is now U.S. Hwy. 70. In 1887 the Maple Hill Seminary building was destroyed by fire and the school discontinued its operations.

*School boy patrol at Highland Heights School.*

Upon the closing of the Maple Hill Seminary, the Lebanon College for Young Ladies opened. The new school grew from 12 students the first year to an enrollment of 145 by 1904. In 1908 the Lebanon College for Young Ladies was sold and its name was changed to Lebanon College and Conservatory.

Mrs. Margaret Harsh in 1891 opened a private school in her home at 326 West Main Street for boys and girls from kindergarten through sixth grade. The school was later transitioned into a high school.

The first free school in Lebanon opened in the former Baptist Seminary building on East Main Street. According to *The Lebanon Herald*, there were 160 students in attendance at the school in 1888. Teachers at the time made an average salary of $30 per month.

In 1902 the site of the former Campbell Academy on North

## The Learning Process, Schools

Cumberland Street was given to the public schools. In a cramped building a professor and seven teachers instructed an enrollment of 600 students at the school with an average daily attendance of 475. The school burned in 1911. The next year a new building was constructed that was sufficiently large enough to accommodate 600 students. The course of study included six grades in the primary and intermediate departments and three high school grades.

In 1936 the entire Lebanon High School facility that occupied a campus at the intersection of North Cumberland and East High (Baddour Parkway) Streets burned. The county moved swiftly to secure replacement buildings for those that had been lost due to the fire. Replacement costs included $106,000 for the main school building, $41,000 for a gymnasium, and $110,000 for an elementary school building.

Almost two decades after moving into the new high school on North Cumberland, it became necessary for the county to build another high school. In 1954 the county let a contract to build a new Lebanon High School on the south side of East Spring Street. The new school was opened in 1955 and cost $610,000 to build.

The old high school was converted to house the 7th and 8th grades and renamed Lebanon Junior High School while the elementary building kept the name Highland Heights.

*Schools integrated in 1961*

Although the federal lawsuit that was to end school segregation, Brown vs. Board of Education of Topeka, Kan., was decided by the U.S. Supreme Court in 1954, it was not until seven years later that schools in Lebanon and Wilson County were desegregated.

In the spring of 1961, the Rev. Cordell Sloan, an African American minister living in Lebanon, enrolled his sons, Cordell Sloan Jr., and Clifford Sloan, in McClain Elementary School. However, both students were denied admission.

*The former Lebanon Junior High School at North Cumberland and Baddour Parkway is now the site of the Wilson County Criminal Justice Center. Before the building served as the Lebanon Junior High it was the Lebanon High School.*

Later in the year, when the fall term was to begin, several African American students attempted to enroll at Lebanon High School but they too were turned away.

Reacting to the local schools' segregation policy, several members of the black community, many of whom were farmers, pooled their financial resources together and hired two legendary Nashville civil rights attorneys, Avon Williams and Z. Alexander Looby, to file a federal lawsuit requiring the schools in Wilson County to be integrated. Their efforts were led for most part by the late Roy Bailey, who lived in Mt. Juliet.

In September 1961, the court ruled in favor of the plaintiffs and the segregation of whites and blacks in schools in Wilson County was brought to an end.

Unlike other communities in the South, local schools were integrated with little disturbance and few incidents.

The late James Bryant became the first black teacher to join the faculty at Lebanon High School and soon after the late Carlos Bruce was named an assistant principal at LHS.

The late Hattie Bryant, wife of James Bryant, was persuaded to take a faculty post at the Lebanon Junior High School in 1964. She taught there for 13 years before retiring. "Miss Hattie," as her students affectionately called her, taught at the all black Market Street Elementary in Lebanon for 20 years before transferring to the Lebanon Junior High.

Her presence and contributions to education and local schools led the Lebanon Special School District to place her name along with that of the late Cordell Winfree, a former district superintendent, on a new middle school in 2011. The school was named Winfree Bryant Middle School.

*City excels in education*

With respect to the topic of education, Lebanon has excelled in both the public and private sectors. In recent years local public schools have received high marks for graduation rates and other student achievements and have been cited as being among the best in Tennessee.

There are currently two private K-12 schools serving Lebanon, Friendship Christian School and McClain Christian Academy; a private pre-K through 5th grade school, Cedars Preparatory Academy; a private university, Cumberland; one public high school, Lebanon High School; and several schools under the administration of the Lebanon Special School District. And for some 60 years there existed Castle Heights Military Academy.

*Lebanon High School.*

## Notes from Lebanon's First 200 Years

*Cumberland University*

Cumberland University, a private and independent school, has an illustrious history dating back to its beginning in 1842.

Cumberland was founded by the Cumberland Presbyterian Church, which in 1847 made the decision to add a school of law to its academic curricula. The Cumberland Law School was the first in Tennessee and the first west of the Appalachian Mountains. In 1854, the Presbyterians added a school of theology.

The original Cumberland Administration building, located on South College Street only a few blocks from where the campus is today, housed the schools of art, law and theology. The building was designed by Philadelphia architect William Strickland, who also designed the

*At the corner of North Greenwood and West Main Street there is a historical marker recognizing that it was on this site that Cumberland's Caruthers' Hall once stood. Known as the "Law Barn," the magnificent building housed the university's prestigious law school. On the site now stands a branch of First Tennessee Bank.*

## The Learning Process, Schools

Tennessee State Capitol and a number of other nationally recognized structures. The building was burned by Union soldiers near the end of the Civil War.

> **AGREEMENT AND BILL OF SALE**
>
> For and in consideration of the sum of One Hundred Twenty-five Thousand Dollars ($125,000.00) cash in hand paid by Howard College of Birmingham, Alabama, to Cumberland University of Lebanon, Tennessee, the receipt of which is hereby acknowledged, Cumberland University does hereby sell, transfer, convey and assign to Howard College the following property:
>
> (1) All of the law books, including, but not limited to, the National Reporter System, the American Digest System, various State Reports and Codes, textbooks, dictionaries, digests, looseleaf volumes, and periodicals belonging to the Law Library at Cumberland University and located in the Law Library in Caruthers Hall on West Main Street in Lebanon, Tennessee.
>
> (2) All of the alumni lists and other records pertaining to the law alumni of Cumberland University; all of the dean's office records; and all of the class pictures of graduates of the Law School of Cumberland University located in Caruthers Hall.
>
> (3) Portrait of the Honorable Cordell Hull, former Secretary of State, presently hung in Caruthers Hall.
>
> (4) All of the funds held by Cumberland University in what is known as the "Green Chair of Law" presently held by Cumberland University in its general funds or endowment funds amounting to approximately $2,300.00.
>
> (5) Any and all right, title and interest that Cumberland University or the Trustees of Cumberland University have in and to a certain trust fund created by the will of Mrs. Mary Martin Brown and presently held by the

*The Bill of Sale for the Cumberland Law School. Sale price of $125,00 shown on Second line of document.*

Notes from Lebanon's First 200 Years

Among the prominent members of the university's faculty following the Civil War was Confederate Gen. A.P. Stewart, who taught at Cumberland as part of a post war parole agreement with the Union. Stewart, who was a professor of mathematics and experimental philosophy, eventually left Cumberland, moved to Mississippi, and in 1874 was named Chancellor of the University of Mississippi, a post he held for a dozen years.

Cumberland's academic reputation, particularly that of its law school, was often touted to be equal to that of Harvard and other prestigious schools in the northeast. As late as the early to mid-1970s, Cumberland was said to be second to only Harvard in having the greatest number of alumni serving in the U.S. Congress.

Cumberland struggled through the years of the Civil War. The school's University Hall was burned by Confederate forces after which a

*Nearing the end of construction in what's likely 1892 or 1893 is Cumberland's Memorial Hall.*

The Learning Process, Schools

student, finding a charred and ruined Corinthian column, inscribed on the column the Latin phrase Ex Cineribus Resurgam (From the ashes I will arise). The university thereafter adopted the mythical phoenix bird as its symbol.

In 1892, Cumberland's Memorial Hall was completed and the university made a final move to the campus on which it exists today.

Cumberland saw a major economic challenge during the Great Depression but woefully managed to stay afloat while many other private schools nationwide were forced to close.

More change and challenges faced the university when the U.S. War Department declared in 1942 that a number of Middle Tennessee counties had been designated to host military training exercises for the Second Army to prepare troops for deployment to battlefields in Europe during World War II.

Wilson County was on the list with several other neighboring counties and Cumberland was selected to be the headquarters host site for the Second Army. Memorial Hall was transitioned into military offices, dormitories housed soldiers, and much of the campus was dotted with tents that also served as housing for troops. The school remained open during this time, but the line between academics and military affairs was often difficult to negotiate. Before the period of maneuvers ended, almost two years, there would be as many as 850,000 soldiers trained in Middle Tennessee for battle.

The Tennessee Baptist Convention assumed control of Cumberland after World War II in 1946, a move that marked the end of a 100-year reign over the university by the Cumberland Presbyterian Church.

In 1951, the Tennessee Baptists closed the College of Arts and Sciences and operated only the School of Law. In 1956, the Cumberland Board of Trust secured an amendment to the Charter and changed Cumberland to a private, independent corporation. As a result, the College of Arts and Sciences was reopened as a two-year junior college, known as Cumberland College of Tennessee.

Faced with a number of demands by the American Bar Association regarding faculty and library contributions that would be too expensive for the university to meet, the Board of Trust made the decision to sell the assets of the law school in 1962 to Howard University in Birmingham, now recognized as Samford University.

It was a different time then than now. Cumberland's financial resources were sparse.

The prestigious law school that had once produced scores of high-profile government officials, members of the state and federal judiciary, and hundreds of well-respected attorneys was sold for $125,000.

The junior college, faced with competition from state owned two-year schools, continued to operate but it too teetered on the edge of financial disaster. Dr. Ernest L Stockton, Jr., whose father had been president of Cumberland from 1926 to 1941, kept the school's doors open during this ever so trying era.

Some 28 years after becoming a junior college, the Board of Trust made the bold move of reverting Cumberland back to a four-year university. Some of the school's trustees disagreed with the decision and resigned from the board, while a contingent of younger members of the board argued it was the only decision that could be made if there was to be a sustainable future for Cumberland.

In a special called meeting on January 26, 1982 the Board of Trust voted in favor of returning Cumberland to four-year status and reviving the name Cumberland University. In 1983, Bob Clement, the son of a former Tennessee governor who was an alumnus of Cumberland, was selected the school's president. The young Clement, after a five-year stint, resigned from Cumberland and was elected to Congress representing Nashville's 5th Congressional District.

Since its resurgence as a four-year university, Cumberland has maintained accreditation with the Southern Association of Accredited

Schools; has established the Jeanette C. Rudy School of Nursing, one of the region's most renowned nursing programs; offers more than 100 programs of study, including eight graduate programs; and anticipates a record enrollment for fall 2019 of about 2,600 students.

For student life on campus the university provides 55 student organizations including three sororities and five fraternities.

Cumberland has also excelled on athletic fields. The school's baseball program in recent years, under the direction of Coach Woody Hunt, has won three national NAIA championships and has been a runner-up twice.

Cumberland is also remembered for suffering the worst defeat ever in college football when in 1916 a Georgia Tech team coached by the legendary John Heisman defeated Cumberland by a score of 222-0. The university is quick to point out that Cumberland did not field a football team in 1916 and that a group of Kappa Sigma fraternity brothers went to Atlanta to play Heisman's team to fulfill a contractual obligation and to keep their beloved school from being sued for breach of contract. A popular book about the game, "Heisman's First Trophy," was published in 2016.

However, before this date Cumberland was considered a powerhouse among college teams in the South. In 1903, Cumberland's football team scored wins over Vanderbilt, Sewanee, Alabama, LSU, Tulane and played a Heisman coached Clemson team to an 11-11 tie in a bowl game played on Thanksgiving Day.

There have been 27 presidents of Cumberland. Dr. Paul C Stumb, IV, has been president of Cumberland since 2015.

The following page includes a list of the past 27 presidents of the university.

# Notes from Lebanon's First 200 Years

*Cumberland Presidents*

Franceway Ranna Cossitt, 1842–44
Thomas C. Anderson, 1844–66
Benjamin W. McDonnold, 1866–73
Nathan Green, Jr., 1873–1902
David Earle Mitchell, 1902–06
Nathan Green, Jr. (Acting), 1906–09
Winstead Paine Bone, 1909–14
Samuel Andrew Coile, 1914–16
Homer Allin Hill (Acting), 1916–17
Edward Powell Childs, 1917–20
Andrew Blake Buchanan (Acting), 1920–22
John Royal Harris, 1922–26
Ernest Looney Stockton, 1926–41
Laban Lacy Rice, 1941–46
Edwin Smith Preston, 1946–50
W. Edwin Richardson, 1950–52
Sam B. Gilreath, 1952–56
Charles B. Havens, 1956–58
Ernest Looney Stockton Jr., 1958–83
Robert N. Clement, 1983–88
M. Walker Buckalew, 1988–91
J. Thomas Mills, 1991–92
Ray C. Phillips, 1992–95
Clair Martin, 1995–2000
Charlene Kozy, 2000–04
Harvill C. Eaton, 2004–15
Paul C. Stumb IV, 2015 – present

*Castle Heights Military Academy*

Founded in 1902, Castle Heights was a premier military prep school in Lebanon for more than 60 years attracting students to fill ranks in the cadet corps from across most of the U.S. and many foreign countries, particularly several countries in South and Central America.

Dr. David Mitchell, a former president of Cumberland University, Isaac W. P. Buchanan, a mathematics professor, A. W. Hooker, a Lebanon businessman, and Dr. Laban L. Rice, an English professor and also a former Cumberland president, were responsible for opening Castle Heights.

Founded in 1902, Castle Heights, at the insistence of its organizers, was first a premier co-educational preparatory school.

It was not until some 16 years later that the school, located less than two miles west of Lebanon's Square, was transformed into an all male military academy.

Castle Heights was just one of what later would become several schools of its type in the South.

Heights, a name for which locals addressed the school, became

The Learning Process, Schools

*Cadets stand in formation on a rainy Sunday afternoon before a scheduled 4 o'clock parade.*

renown for recruiting and attracting students to fill ranks in its cadet corps from virtually every state in the U.S. and many foreign countries to include several countries in South and Central America and a number of the island territories in the Caribbean.

Originally the school was coeducational but became an all male military preparatory school in 1918 as a result of World War I. In 1970, in an effort to beef-up enrollment, policy was changed and Heights began admitting female students once again.

Castle Heights was acquired for $100,000 in 1928 by Benarr McFadden, an eccentric wealthy New York businessman who owned hotels, restaurants, commercial real estate, and publishing companies. McFadden had an international reputation for his health conscious beliefs relating to food and exercise. He once ran for mayor of New York City, the U.S. Senate, and U.S. President, all unsuccessfully.

In March 1931, because of a special relationship that McFadden shared with Italy's Fascist dictator, Benito Mussolini, 45 young Italian men were deployed by Mussolini to attend school at Castle Heights for three months. They came to learn about military training and McFadden's exercise and nutrition programs.

At one time, shortly after the mid-1950s, Castle Heights had an enrollment of near 600 students, many of whom were boarding students living on campus. For several years an academic curriculum was offered for first through twelfth grades.

*Castle Heights 1902-03 football team.*

As enrollment began to decline in the 1970s, the school struggled to stay afloat. Many blamed the Vietnam War for tarnishing the popularity of the military and making attending a private military academy a not so attractive option for a preparatory school and therefore the demise of Castle Heights. Heights closed in 1986.

There still exists in Lebanon coveted remembrances about Castle Heights. About the public audiences that would gather on campus to

*Spring formal dance at Castle Heights.*

watch Sunday afternoon parades - always at 4 o'clock - and about the special Easter parade in which cadets would break out their spring white uniforms complete with cross belts and marching in-step as they shouldered heavy M-1 rifles.

And it was always a delight for locals to see young cadets, many high school age but others in early elementary grades, marching to church in formation on Sunday mornings rain or shine. The cadet corps routinely marched in the town's Christmas parade and its band and drill team made frequent appearances at events in other cities such as the Cotton Carnival in Memphis.

*Castle Heights bugler.*

Although there is no school remaining on what was originally a sprawling 150-acre campus, there are still standing several of the school's original buildings. What was the school's administration building, mess hall and barracks for some students, "Main," is now fully restored and serves as City Hall for the City of Lebanon. The former home of the Castle Heights president is today a popular restaurant, Sammy B's; and the school library is owned by the Castle Heights Alumni Association which uses the space as an operations center for the alumni organization. A few other structures remain on campus and are used as office buildings.

The Mitchell House, which graces the front of the campus on West Main Street, was built by Dr. David Mitchell, who was president of Cumberland University at the time. Construction began on the Neo-Classical Revival Style mansion in 1906 and was completed in 1910. Mitchell brought in special craftsmen to build the home and imported chandeliers from Italy and carpets from Austria as part of the furnishings.

After being used as the Mitchell family residence, the structure, containing 10,600 sq. ft. of living space when built, served as the headquarters for the junior school and barracks for some junior school cadets.

More than 20 years ago and about 12 years after Heights closed, the Mitchell House was completely renovated and used as the headquarters offices for the holding company of Cracker Barrel Old Country Store, Inc. from 1998 to 2013. More recently the mansion, which is listed on the U.S. National Register of Historic Places, has served as the international headquarters for Sigma Pi fraternity. It was acquired by the City of Lebanon in 2019 and is to be used for offices.

*The Mitchell House.*

Among the more famous alumni of Castle Heights are Gregg and Duane Allman, founders of the Allman Brothers Band; Lt. Gen. John A. Bradley, U.S. Air Force, Commander of U.S. Air Force Reserve Command; Gen. Wesley Clark, U.S. Army and presidential candidate; Dan Evins, co-founder Cracker Barrel Old Country Store, Inc.; Gen.

*Castle Heights Main, now Lebanon's City Hall.*

The Learning Process, Schools

Lance Lord, U.S. Air Force, Commander of the Air Force Space Command; Pete Rademacher, heavyweight boxer; Herbert S. Walters, U.S. Senator from Tennessee; and John Wyeth Chandler, mayor of Memphis.

*Lebanon Special School District*

Since 1901, albeit under a different name, there has been a Lebanon city school system. Initially it was the Special Tenth District Lebanon City Schools and today the name is Lebanon Special School District.

Created by a special act of the state legislature, the original legislation called for a three-member school board to govern the school district and that board members would be elected at large by the voters of the district with each serving a term of six years. On staggered terms of office, one board member is elected every two years at the time of local general elections.

The Lebanon Special School District's mission is "committed to a community of excellence."

The district provides instruction for pre-kindergarten through eighth grade, as well as, services for children qualifying for special education.

Funding for the city school system comes from four revenue sources including the State of Tennessee Basic Education Program (BEP) allocation, a percentage of Wilson County property tax collections and sales tax receipts, and the Lebanon Special School District property tax. The Act of 1901 instituted that a tax would be levied on properties in the district in support of the operation of schools.

Schools in the Lebanon Special School District include Byars Dowdy Elementary, Coles Ferry Elementary, Sam Houston Elementary, Castle Heights Elementary, Walter J. Baird Middle School, and Winfree Bryant Middle School.

## Notes from Lebanon's First 200 Years

*'Special Needs' education introduced*

In 1949, the late Mr. and Mrs. Willis H. (Tex) Maddox introduced a "special needs" educational program in Lebanon before most of the state and region was even aware that there was a need for such an initiative.

They opened their home on West Spring Street to provide educational opportunities for a handful of students with various disabilities. The special education classes were later taken from the Maddox home and placed in McClain School on West Main and soon after that a special education program was started at Highland Heights.

*Lebanon High School*

The only school located in Lebanon that falls under the guidance of the Wilson County Board of Education is the Lebanon High School.

In 2012, LHS moved into a new modern facility on a spacious campus on South Hartmann Drive. Boasting an enrollment of almost 2,000 students, the school maintains a graduation rate in the mid-90s and ranks among the best in Tennessee.

The school on South Hartmann Drive is the third place of residence for Lebanon High School dating back to a location on North Cumberland Street where in 1902 the property of a private school, Campbell Academy, was given to the public school system. It was on this site that the first Lebanon High School was chartered in 1918.

It wasn't until 1955 that Lebanon High School was moved to a second facility off East Spring Street on Harding Drive. While a number of additions and makeovers were necessary to accommodate increases in enrollment and technology demands, the second Lebanon High School remained in service for 57 years.

The former structure, built in 1955, was reopened in 2018 as a state-of-the-art administrative and training complex for the Wilson County Board of Education.

The mission adopted by Lebanon High "is to challenge all students to

The Learning Process, Schools

exceed educational standards through rigorous courses of study that are relevant to real-world applications and to encourage students to develop positive relationships through varied interests, which will inspire them to be productive and successful citizens."

*Wilson County Training School*

Long before the 1960s and before all white schools were ordered by federal courts to accept black students through a process called mandated integration, there were all black schools.

In Lebanon there were two African American schools before integration, Wilson County Training School and Market Street Elementary.

After the Civil War, the state legislature passed a law requiring all schools to be free. Students must be allowed to attend without having to pay tuition. The new law applied to both black and white students saying schools must be as "free as air to all of legal age."

So, with the new law and with a disdain for mixing black and white students in the same school and classroom, separate schools were built for black students.

Wilson County Training School, later recognized as Wilson County High School, was built in 1923 and located on Market Street.

The school remained in service until 1969. Even after Lebanon High School had been integrated some African American students preferred to finish their high school years where they started and remained at Wilson County High School until the school closed.

On the same property with the Wilson County High School was also Market Street Elementary.

The high school building was torn down in 2000 but Market Street Elementary was saved and used for a neighborhood community center.

For some 46 years Wilson County High School educated its own under a doctrine whites boasted as separate but equal.

Although the truth of the matter was that black schools and white schools were separate but in no way could they be considered equal. Black schools were the stepchildren of white schools. Black schools got second hand books, used musical equipment for their bands and other hand-me-down materials.

A.C. Wharton, Jr., the former Mayor of the City of Memphis and Shelby County and a product of Wilson County High School said at a reunion of the school in 2014 when speaking about the teachers who taught there, "They didn't have much. But they did a heck of a lot with what they did have." And he added, "It isn't what you have, but it's what you do with what you have."

Wilson County Training School principals included Harrison Jarrett, Albert Moore, Joe Thomas, James Bryant and Carlos Bruce.

Bryant became the first African American to join the Lebanon High School faculty in 1964 and Bruce became an assistant principal at LHS when the Wilson County Training School closed. Bryant's wife, Miss Hattie as she was known throughout the community, left Market Street Elementary in 1964 for a teaching position at Lebanon Junior High School.

*Friendship Christian School*

In 1973, Friendship Christian School began classes in temporary facilities at College Street Church of Christ under the direction of the late Leonard K. Bradley and with substantial financial support from the late Dr. Sam B. McFarland and other Lebanon businessmen.

Col. Bradley, recognized as Friendship's academic and administrative leader, was well known in the community, had an excellent reputation for his work as a school administrator as a result of his decades of service at Castle Heights Military Academy as that school's headmaster. His appointment at Friendship gave the new school immediate credibility.

Starting another private school in a small community where there already existed a private school that had been in operation for 70 years, Castle Heights Military Academy, was a bold if not a high-risk venture.

But it was one Dr. McFarland and Col. Bradley were willing to accept in order to provide a choice to parents within the community desiring to send their children to a private school with an emphasis on Christian education.

The original Friendship board included Dr. McFarland, Kenneth O. Lester, Jr. (his son Kevin Lester is the current Friendship board Chairman), Jack Hendrickson, Steve Botts, and E.W. (Eddie) Evins. All of the original board members are deceased except for Botts.

Friendship, which now offers a K3-12th grade curriculum of study, moved to its current 50-acre campus just north of Lebanon on Coles Ferry Pike in 1976.

The school has a total enrollment of about 700 students and maintains an 11:1 teacher to student ratio.

Friendship has a number of accomplishments related to the classroom as well as the athletic field.

The average ACT score among graduating students is 25.2, 28 among the top 50 percent of the graduation class, 29.5 among the top 25 percent, and 31 among the top 10 percent. Friendship offers students college credit hours through a dual enrollment program with Lipscomb University and also offers a number of Advanced Placement courses.

Through 2019, the Friendship Commanders have scored 21 state athletic championships including 3 in football and baseball, 10 in bowling, 2 in volleyball, and 1 each in basketball, softball and cross-country.

Explaining Friendship's role today, school President Jon Shoulders writes, "At Friendship Christian School, we exist to instill knowledge, faith, love, and compassion into the minds and hearts of our students. We believe that offering exceptional academics, arts, athletics, and service, presented through a Christian world-view, is vital in preparing our students for all aspects of life."

*McClain Christian Academy*

Accepting students from Pre-K through the 8th grade, McClain Christian Academy is committed to academic excellence in a Christian environment.

Located on U.S. Hwy. 70 in Lebanon, MCA McClain Christian Academy is a Category 1 school approved by the Tennessee Department of Education. The school follows rules and regulations mandated by the state of Tennessee, teachers are licensed by the state, and the curriculum offered by MCA is aligned with Tennessee state standards.

According to a statement on the MCA website, the school's administration continually analyzes curriculum so that the advanced academic courses offered are providing students with the best possible education.

A focal point at MCA is providing students individualized instruction within the small class structure to ensure that each student excels not only academically but socially as well.

*McClain Elementary School on West Main Street where today is located an attorney's office and Cedars Prepatory Academy.*

MCA is a nonprofit 501c(3) entity that was incorporated in 2006. Dr. Paul M. Graden is the headmaster at MCA.

*Cedars Preparatory Academy*

Nestled among trees on a site off West Main Street that once was a portion of the campus occupied by one of Lebanon's foremost elementary schools, McClain School, now stands Cedars Preparatory Academy, or as it is more commonly known, Cedars Prep.

Mary Beard, who holds a Masters Degree in Education, is the founder of Cedars Prep. Years ago she had a vision to create a one-of-a-kind private school to serve younger ages and the plan and program she developed has made a lasting mark on education in Lebanon.

Her 30-years of experience in the field of education, including some two decades as a school director and owner, has made it possible for her to create a very unique private school on a generous campus that is housed in a spacious modern facility.

Cedars Prep offers a preschool and kindergarten curriculum with both year-round and traditional nine month programs, as well as elementary grades 1st through 5th, and summer programs for ages two through twelve. Also a part of Cedars Prep is the Owl's Nest, a program provided for ages six weeks to 2-years.

# Chapter Nine
# Those Who Healed the Community

Unlike many other communities its size, Lebanon in its early years was fortunate to have a reputable health care community forged with physicians with medical degrees from ranking universities in the northeast as well as nearby Vanderbilt and the former University of Nashville, which was acquired by the University of Tennessee.

And there were also others, some called doctors, who worked to heal the sick but not necessarily with knowledge they gained from a medical school classroom but instead with homespun remedies passed down from one generation to another.

One of Lebanon's first settlers, Nettie Jacobs, is credited with healing several area residents who had become sick from a cholera epidemic during the 1830s. It was reported that the treatment he administered to his patients, which involved a concoction of herbs, he had learned from living in an Indian tribe as a young boy.

Since the early 1800s, Lebanon has been a chief provider of health care for many from nearby rural communities, particularly small towns and counties north and east of Lebanon. This was the case in 1894 when Dr. R.Q. Lillard opened an infirmary at 323 West Main Street and has continued to be the case in more modern times.

As recently as 2015, Macon County, about 35 miles northeast of Lebanon, was second to Wilson County in having the greatest number of patients filling beds at the Lebanon hospital. While Lebanon has attracted patients from other areas for more than 100 years, it continues to be the practice even more so today as the hospital and local medical community provide a number of highly reputable specialty care cohorts to include orthopedics, cardiology, neurology, radiology, oncology, obstetrics, general and cardiovascular surgery, psychiatric care, and others.

*Military service*

Over Lebanon's 200 years several local physicians gained recognition for their skills and talents in treating the sick and many for their selfless and heroic service to the nation's military.

Dr. Samuel Hogg, described in the "History of Wilson County" as a "soldier, financier, statesman, and physician," was one of city's first five commissioners appointed by the Tennessee General Assembly in 1807. Hogg, a friend of Andrew Jackson, accompanied Jackson to the Battle of New Orleans and served in Jackson's army as a surgeon. He was also a business partner of Jackson's in one of Lebanon's first retail stores.

Among other local physicians to be called from their practice to serve in the military were Dr. John L. Wynne, who practiced with Dr. Hogg, served in the War of 1812 as regimental surgeon; Dr. William P. Smith was surgeon-general of the Army of Texas; and Dr. James Frazer was also with Jackson at the Battle of New Orleans.

A number of local doctors abandoned their practices and joined the battle cry of the Confederacy to fill the ranks as surgeons and general practitioners during the Civil War. Some actually put away the instruments of their profession and took command of combat units.

A list of local physicians who served with the Confederacy included Drs. John Eskew, James L. Fite, G.W. Huddleston, Joseph Rogers, Oliver Cromwell Kidder, James R. Lester, J.N. Curd, Thomas C. Wheeler, John William McFarland Eskew, G.L. Robertson, William Blythe, John Duncan Estes, J.S. Haralson, William George and R.H. Baker.

Dr. Fite was surgeon of the 7th Tennessee Infantry just before the Battle of Seven Pines where Lebanon's Gen. Robert Hatton was killed.

Also serving in Hatton's 7th were Dr. Lester, as an assistant surgeon, who resigned from his medical duties in 1862 to take command of a Confederate cavalry company, Dr. Blythe, a lieutenant in the 7th, and Dr.

Robertson, a surgeon.

Dr. Curd was an assistant surgeon and medical steward for the 45th Tennessee as was Dr. Kidder. Dr. Wheeler served as a surgeon for the 16th Tennessee and Dr. McFarland was an officer in the 4th Tennessee Cavalry Regiment.

Records show that Dr. Huddleston served as a surgeon in the Confederate Army, Dr. Haralson with the 2nd Tennessee Cavalry, and that Dr. Estes served in the Confederacy.

Dr. Baker entered military service with the Confederate Army at age 16 and was taken prisoner twice. Also captured during the war, but held only briefly were Drs. Robertson and Fite.

Dr. R.L.C. White served in the Confederacy and after the war attended Nashville Medical College, then Jefferson Medical College in Philadelphia and returned to Lebanon to practice until 1882 at which time he vacated his practice and served as editor of *The Lebanon Herald*.

Lebanon physicians who served in uniform in World War II included Col. O. Reed Hill, Lt. Col. James P. Leathers, Maj. Kenneth Tilley, and Capt. Thomas Richard Puryear.

Others who served in the Army Medical Corps, according to the "History of Wilson County" were Drs. John Holmes Peyton, James McFarland, Charles Williamson, Robert Thompson, who was the 100th Infantry Medical Inspector in Germany.

Dr. Charles L. Kirkpatrick, entered the Medical Corps in 1929, rose to the rank of colonel and commanded the great general hospital in Tokyo for several years after the war including during a period of the Korean War. He returned to the U.S. and was placed in command of the hospital at Ft. Belvoir in Washington, D.C.

Dr. Robert Haralson was the first Lebanon medical officer credited as a medical paratroop.

Dr. A.T. Hall was on active duty with the U.S. Air Force during the Korean War and afterwards returned to McFarland Hospital as a surgeon.

Notes from Lebanon's First 200 Years

There have been several Lebanon physicians who have served in the military in recent times and perhaps one of the most prominent on this list is the late Dr. Joe Frank Bryant, who in 1965 volunteered to join a government sponsored program, Project Vietnam, and spent three months as a surgeon in DaNang, South Vietnam.

His role as a surgeon treating wounded U.S. soldiers was recognized in a best-selling book, "The Green Berets." Before his volunteer duty in Vietnam, Dr. Bryant served two years in the Navy.

Dr. Bryant, a former chairman of the Cumberland University Board of Trust, owned a local television station, WJFB, which was designated by the Federal Communications Commission as a "must carry" station meaning the station's programming was required to be carried by a local cable provider. In the case of WJFB the "must carry" rule meant the station had access to several hundred thousand homes in Middle Tennessee which were all subscribers to the same cable provider.

Dr. Thomas R. Puryear, who maintained a general practice on East Main Street from the mid-1950s to the 1970s, served as a captain in the army during World War II.

Other Lebanon physicians and dentists who have served in the military include Drs. Robert C. Bone, Greg White, John Kane, Dwayne Lett, Russell Kirk, Wayne Johnson, and Paul Nawiesniak.

*Many had other jobs, served in other ways*

Besides attending to the community's sick, many of the early local physicians had other jobs or occupations to help support their families as the practice of medicine was not always so financially rewarding.

Dr. John Owen founded an apothecary shop in Lebanon in 1853 and later served as president of Bank of Wilson County.

Dr. Kidder taught school as did other doctors.

Dr. William Hannah moved to Lebanon in 1885 and opened a feed and livery stable business.

## Those Who Healed the Community

Dr. G.R. Gwynn had medical offices on the Square in 1887 and also operated a drug store.

Dr. H.K. Edgerton opened his practice here in 1893 and later organized the Lebanon Woolen Mills.

Dr. John Owen Campbell, son of Gov. Bowen Campbell, received a medical degree from Vanderbilt, left Lebanon for Austin, Texas and returned here and farmed.

Dr. Miles McCorkle was a state legislator and founding member of the Cumberland University Board of Trust.

Dr. Joseph Mottley Anderson, regarded as the town's first specialist, studied at the University of Pennsylvania Medical School from 1835-37 and at one time was said to have the largest obstetrical practice in state. He also had an ownership interest in several businesses and served as Lebanon's mayor.

And not to help support themselves financially, but other Lebanon doctors have assumed public jobs and served on public boards.

Dr. J.R. Bone, a 1908 graduate of the University of Nashville Medical School, was a member of the county draft board during World War I and also held the post of city health officer.

Dr. R.C. Kash, a local general practitioner, was a member of the county school board and was also the Wilson County coroner.

Dr. O. Reed Hill served on the Lebanon 10th District school board and was elected a member of the county's first library board in 1938.

Dr. Robert Dean Wilkinson, who started his dental practice in Lebanon in 1926, acquired and operated the historic Horn Springs resort.

In 1922, Dr. H.W. Bell became the first African American dentist to practice in Lebanon.

Dr. Gordon Miller, a Lebanon dentist, was elected to the Wilson County Board of Education. He was also an original member of the board of directors of Cracker Barrel Old Country Store, Inc.

Dr. B.S. (Billy) Howard, a local dentist, served on the Lebanon city council and was a member of the Peoples Bank board of directors.

Dr. Robert Givan, began his dental practice in Lebanon in 1958 and was a member of the Lebanon Airport Commission.

Dr. Frank Baddour, a local optometrist, was a native of Beirut, Lebanon. He served on the city council and became the town's first vice mayor as part of a special program making it possible for him to return to his homeland for a visit in a quasi official capacity. Dr. Baddour was involved in a number of civic and community organizations. The Lebanon U.S. Hwy. 70 Bypass, Baddour Parkway, is named in his honor.

*Infirmaries and hospitals*

As mentioned earlier, Dr. R.Q. Lillard opened a Lebanon infirmary in 1894. Eight years later in 1902 Dr. H.K. Edgerton built Edgerton's Infirmary on South College Street.

Edgerton's Infirmary became Cedarcroft Sanitarium, an institution created to treat drug addiction as a disease. Also at the time a facility was opened on West Main, Cumberland Sanitarium, with a similar practice regarding addiction. Cumberland Sanitarium burned in 1915.

The structure that housed Cedarcroft Sanitarium became Martha Gaston Hospital in 1932. Dr. R.B. Gaston launched the hospital after leaving his practice and management responsibilities at the already established McFarland Hospital. He named the hospital in memory of his mother.

Today the Martha Gaston hospital building, after a number of improvements and additions, remains intact and is operated as a nonprofit providing housing for men with disabilities under the name Cedarcroft. T.A. Bryan, other local businessmen, and church leaders opened Cedarcroft in 1974.

Martha Gaston Hospital began to shutter its operations in the mid-1960s, but the building was soon acquired by Bryan and reconfigured to house Bryan's Insurance agency, other professional offices and start-up

Lebanon businesses. Also remaining in the building with their medical practices were Drs. Reed Hill Tilley and Roscoe Kash, who had been associated with the Martha Gaston Hospital for a number of years. Dr. Harvey Grime, a radiologist, also kept offices there.

The Tilley family, starting with Dr. L.L. Tilley and later his sons Drs. John Hill Tilley and Dr. Kenneth Tilley, were largely responsible for the management and ongoing operations at Martha Gaston. After the hospital ceased operations, the Tilleys continued to practice medicine in Lebanon and sent their patients to McFarland Hospital.

*Martha Gaston Hospital on South College Street now owned by Cedar Croft.*

Dr. L.L. Tilley practiced medicine for 45 years, first in Tucker's Crossroads and then in Lebanon. His two sons opened their practices here in 1940 at the time of their father's death.

*McFarland Hospital*

McFarland Hospital was founded by Dr. Sam Walker McFarland in 1917 at the corner of Park Avenue and East Spring Street. The first building contained ten patient rooms, an operating room, kitchen and dining room.

The first McFarland to practice medicine here was Dr. James Harvey McFarland in 1841. Following him was his son John William and then his two sons Jerry and Sam Walker McFarland.

It was Dr. Sam B. McFarland, often with a cigar extending from the corner of his mouth, who did most of the surgeries and ran the business of McFarland Hospital for decades.

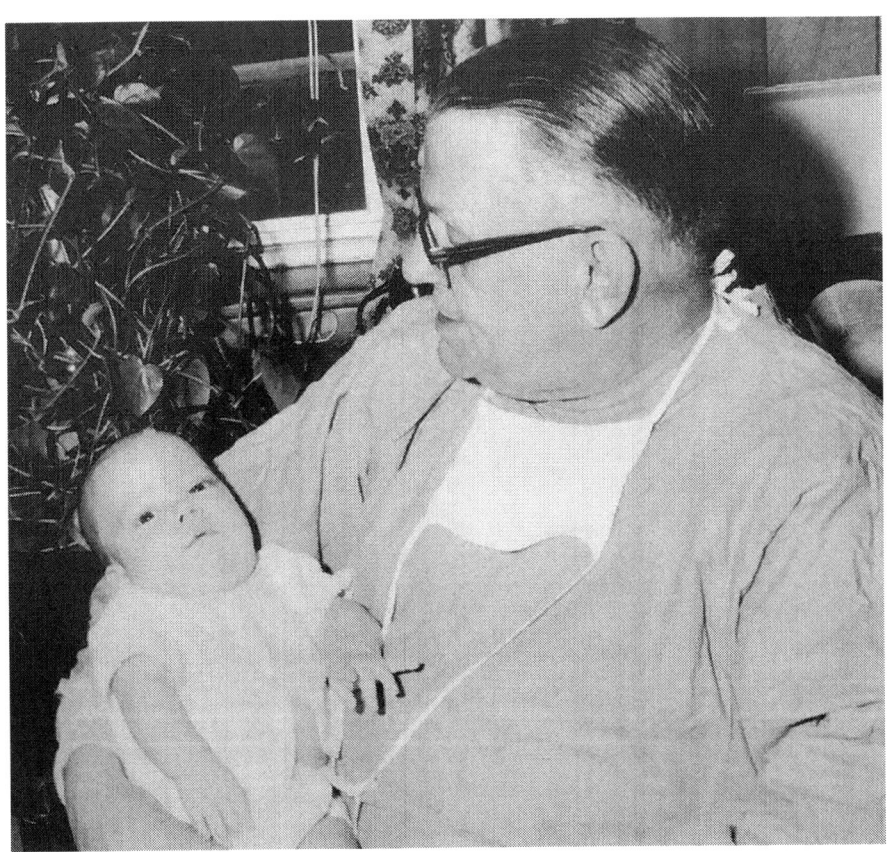

*Dr. Sam McFarland holds a newborn.*

He was an icon in health care in Lebanon and Wilson County and for that matter much of Middle Tennessee.

Noted for patrolling the halls of his hospital and visiting from patient room to patient room - in the earlier years with a stogie sometimes lit but in the latter years just a non-threatening fixture wedged between his lips in the corner of his mouth - "Dr. Sam," as he was known in the community, was a philanthropist, businessman, family doctor and general surgeon. And he was one of Lebanon's and, many would say, the state's most influential citizens.

Politicians running for local and state offices would aggressively seek his public endorsement. Charities stood at his door for a generous contribution. And many were awestruck just to be in his presence. Friendship Christian School was founded as a result of his benevolence and influence.

He was indeed the face and name affixed to McFarland Hospital. "Dr. Sam" sold McFarland Hospital in the late 1970s to the Humana Corporation.

The sale of McFarland to Humana came shortly after ground was broken in 1977 for the new University Medical Center Hospital on Baddour Parkway.

*University Medical Center*

It was a cool fall day on October 17, 1977, when a delegation gathered for a groundbreaking ceremony on what would become the front lawn of University Medical Center Hospital.

Among those standing behind a plow being dragged by a white mule were Albert Gore, Jr., who would be taking office in January as a freshman Congressman; the late Yvonne Wallace, a UMC board member and business manager of The Lebanon Democrat; and Jack McGaw, UMC board chairman and plant manager at TRW Ross Gear.

UMC was an idea conceived by Dr. Robert Carver Bone, a young 40-year-old doctor at the time, whose family was prominent in a number of circles in Wilson County including business, agriculture, politics and education.

Dr. Bone, a popular family physician and general surgeon, who like a lot of small town doctors found that his practice covered a broad swath from treating minor head colds to delivering babies to delicate and serious surgeries, gathered public support across the community to establish a new state-of-the-art regional hospital.

*Lebanon's University Medical Center now owned by Vanderbilt Healthcare.*

His plan would be for the not-for-profit hospital to be governed by a local board and to return a generous financial contribution annually to Cumberland University, where he served on the Board of Trust along with his father Sam Stratton Bone and later his brother Harold Gordon Bone. The latter Bone served as the administrator/chief executive officer at UMC for about a year and a half before UMC was sold to American Health Corp.

Dr. Bone carefully chose influential folk in the community to help move his idea forward including the manager of the town's largest employer, TRW; a principal in the community's local newspaper; and others.

In 1979, two years after the groundbreaking ceremony, the hospital opened.

The idea of starting a second hospital in Lebanon did not come without controversy.

Members of the health care profession and others loyal to Dr. Sam McFarland and his hospital viewed Dr. Bone's efforts with respect to establishing a second hospital in Lebanon as disrespectful and challenging to the "old guard" in the local medical community.

Soon lines were drawn. Some physicians vowed to not leave McFarland Hospital under any circumstances, others tried to practice at both facilities, and then there were those who practiced only at UMC and would not go across town to McFarland.

The struggle and competition between the two hospitals separated the community in a number of ways beyond just the practice of medicine. Both hospitals had local boards. The rhetoric between the two institutions was often degrading and frequently forced decisions that caused further divisiveness in the community.

Two sales changed much of this.

First McFarland Hospital was sold to Humana only a couple of years after the start-up of UMC.

And then in 1982 UMC was sold to American Healthcorp, a Nashville based health care company, whose two principals were Robert Hilton, a member of the Cracker Barrel board at that time, and Tom Ciggaran, who later chaired American Healthways, the name adopted by American Healthcorp in 1999, and an owner and recent chairman of the Nashville Predators professional ice hockey team.

The sale of UMC resulted in a gift to Cumberland University in the form of a trust fund in the amount of $1.1 million and the commitment of a $50,000 gift annually for 99 years.

In 1984 American Healthcorp made the decision to divest its interests in hospitals and sold UMC in Lebanon to Tenet Health Care.

It was this transaction that finally caused a consolidation of the two hospitals and brought Lebanon's health care community together.

A leading personality in all of this was Larry Keller, a hospital administrator brought to Lebanon by Humana in 1983 to run McFarland Hospital. Keller soon proved his worth at McFarland and was lured across town to UMC to be that facility's chief executive officer.

The trail opened by Keller to UMC was soon followed by physicians at McFarland who had been reluctant, because of personal loyalties, to go across town to the new hospital.

In 1989 Humana sold McFarland to Tenet and the operations of the two hospitals were merged.

With Keller already there and McFarland's flag flying now with Tenet and UMC, the local medical community was together.

Doctors who had been at McFarland but moved their privileges to UMC included the popular family physician, Dr. James C. Bradshaw, a relative of Dr. Sam McFarland; Dr. Stephen Neely, Lebanon's first orthopedic surgeon who came here from Boston, Massachusetts; Dr. Jimmy Morris, a Castle Heights graduate from Lebanon and general surgeon; Dr. Morris Ferguson, a family practitioner; Dr. Hardie Sorrels, a general practice physician and Lebanon High School graduate whose family owned a local pharmacy; and others.

Keller's influence on health care in Lebanon encouraged the recruitment of many more specialists and placed a greater emphasis on the hospital's mission to serve a region comprised of more than a dozen counties.

Other orthopedists were recruited to the local hospital including Drs. Roy Terry, Paul Abbey, Charles (Bob) Kaelin, Damon Petty, and Jon Cornelius, the first surgeon in Tennessee to adopt robotic joint replacement of the knee and hip.

But also joining the ranks of specialists at the hospital were cardiologists, Drs. Robert Woods and Kathleen Kearney-Gray; obstetricians, Drs. Charles Lanning and Alan Roundtree; ENT-otolaryngologist, Dr. John Tate; neurologist, Dr. Wiaam Falouji; physiatrists, Drs. Scott Baker and Jeffrey Hazlewood; and podiatrist, Dr. Yong Suh.

The McFarland campus became a physical rehab site and was designated to house a psychiatric program. Both of which are maintained by UMC. Cumberland University's Jeanette C. Rudy School of Nursing is also located in the McFarland building.

Since Tenet, owners of UMC have included Health Management Associates, a Florida company; Community Health Systems, headquartered in Franklin; and most recently the hospital was purchased by Vanderbilt University Medical Center.

Licensed for 245 beds, the hospital features a plethora of health care specialties. Its economic impact to the local community exceeded $58 million in 2018, including $14 million in charity and uncompensated care. With more than 200 physicians and over 600 employees on staff, the hospital is one of Lebanon's largest employers, with a payroll topping $38 million.

*Renowned African American physician*

Dr. John W. Glover, a graduate of Meharry Medical School in 1932, opened a medical practice in Lebanon and was the only African American physician here for several years extending into the 1960s.

Dr. Glover, who was popular in both the white and black communities, took an active role in a number of community activities and held a financial interest in several local businesses.

He also chaired the Wilson County Negro Fair Association, the group responsible for producing an agricultural and entertainment fair during the 1950s before integration. In 1959, Dr. Glover was vice president of the Wilson County Civic League.

*He delivered more than 14,000 babies*

In this chapter the names of physicians who served in the military are told along with several family names with a renowned lineage in health care including the likes of McFarland, Tilley, Hill, Bone and others.

One name that has not been mentioned is that of Dr. Charles T. Lowe.

On January 16, 1985 the obstetrical unit at UMC was dedicated to Dr. Lowe.

The occasion was marked with an official proclamation issued by Wilson County Executive Don Simpson and the honoree was cited for his contributions to the medical profession and being a "pillar" of the medical community.

Dr. Lowe, a Vanderbilt graduate, was also recognized for delivering more than 14,000 babies during his career in Lebanon while practicing at McFarland and UMC hospitals.

*Despite his hardship*

Dr. Harvey Grime received his degree in medicine in 1959 from the University of Tennessee. He was also named to receive the Charles C. Verstandig Award as the graduate who had to overcome the most obstacles to earn his degree.

Dr. Grime milked cows on his father's farm early in the morning and after dark to get the money necessary to attend college. In medical school he took night jobs and part time work at Memphis hospitals and elsewhere and borrowed money to help with expenses.

After six quarters of study he was stricken with tuberculosis but managed to overcome the disease and returned to school to successfully complete his requirements for graduation.

*Cumberland nursing program*

Playing a prominent role in local health care since it was established in 1992 is the Cumberland University Jeanette C. Rudy School of Nursing.

The university's nursing and health professions program, considered one of the state's most elite, was initiated by the late Jeanette C. Rudy, a registered nurse herself and member of the Cumberland Board of Trust. Her financial contributions as a major benefactor of the university made the nursing program possible. The program was named in her honor in

2004.

Since its origin, the nursing school, housed on the McFarland campus with some 400 students enrolled, has been responsible for filling hundreds of vacancies in the health care field here, in Middle Tennessee, and throughout the U.S.

*Cumberland medical department*

In 1871, the Medical School of Memphis became the Medical Department of Cumberland University.

Cumberland was only affiliated with the Memphis School for two years before terminating its relationship in 1873.

# Chapter Ten
# Potpourri

*World War II maneuvers*

In 1942, Gov. Prentice Cooper announced that the U.S. Army would be conducting tactical training exercises in several Middle Tennessee counties to prepare troops for battle on war fronts in Europe.

Wilson would be one of the counties where the World War II maneuvers would take place, but even more importantly Cumberland University in Lebanon would be designated the Second Army Headquarters for the true-to-life war-like exercises.

For the better part of a two-year period much of Middle Tennessee was engulfed with more than 850,000 soldiers.

The terrain in Middle Tennessee, being much like that of Europe, as well as the climate, were two major contributing factors that led planners of the war in Washington to declare the area ideal for getting troops ready before being shipped out to battlefronts.

Cumberland was selected by the War Department as the headquarters for the Second Army for several reasons. There was adequate office space available in its main administration building, Memorial Hall, to accommodate the Second Army's command cadre. With dormitories available

*Soldiers' tents on Cumberland campus during World War II maneuvers.*

there was an abundance of housing on campus for soldiers and there were also vacant land areas around campus where some soldiers could bivouac in tents. And Cumberland was relatively close to the Lebanon airport and not far from Nashville.

When the initial announcement was made about the military exercises, only nine Middle Tennessee counties were listed to be in the training theatre. However, before the maneuvers ended, 12 more counties were added bringing the total number of participating counties to 21.

*Army gliders fly low over a farm field during World War II maneuvers.*

For Wilson County and the other counties in the training area, life was different during this two-year period.

Farms became battlefields, back roads were transitioned into tank trails, military checkpoints guarded intersections, foxholes were randomly dug in open spaces, and thousands of soldiers patrolled, marched, trained and combed the area.

The lives of locals were intertwined with those of the visiting soldiers. The late Eugene Sloan, who lived in Lebanon during the maneuvers, writes in Chapter 26 of the "History of Wilson County," "Civilians endured the inconvenience of blocked roads, the absence of milk and mail deliveries, delayed school buses,

*Soldiers cross a nearby creek during World War II maneuvers.*

and experienced the dangers of driving along narrow, twisting roads with headlights blacked out. Privacy was forgotten in this land where soldiers tented at night on lawns and in barn lots and fought from house to house through village and farm. The rumble of heavy artillery, the staccato bark of rifle and machine gun fire, the night long eerie growl of tanks, the awesome beauty of thousands of paratroopers pouring from C-47's were all part of living in Wilson County from the summer of 1942 until late spring of 1944."

The late John R. Hatcher, Jr., whose father operated the Princess Theatre a half block off the Square on South Cumberland Street, said he could remember seeing soldiers during maneuvers on the weekend lined-up halfway around the Square and stretching back up East Main Street a

*In 1923 a special promotion was held at the Princess Theatre on South Cumberland Street for the movie Covered Wagon. Standing to the left in the photo is John R. Hatcher, Sr., who operated the Princess, and later with his son John R. Hatcher, Jr., was a co-operator of a second Theatre that opened in Lebanon in 1949, the Capitol. The Capitol Theatre, totally renovated and restored, is owned today by Bob and Pam Black.*

couple of blocks just waiting for the opportunity to get inside the theatre and see a movie. He said they'd stand in line for hours waiting their turn.

When soldiers were off duty, restaurants, stores, churches and any place they could go and be welcomed was packed. Frequently on the weekend school gyms would be opened for fellowship, dinners and dances for soldiers to attend. And often residents would open their homes to soldiers they may have met at church, during a training exercise on their property or under some other circumstance providing them with a home cooked meal and a respite from their military obligations.

The Second Army cooperated as much as possible with civilians when asked to do so. As an example, Col. W.H. Crawford, Second Army Provost Marshal, advised in a story appearing in a 1943 edition of The Lebanon Democrat that "There will be no military exercises or road blackouts during the week of the Wilson County Fair."

The Second Army was reportedly also good to make reparations when private property was lost or damaged because of training exercises. It was not unusual for a tank to plow through a fence row, a gate to be left open and a cow escape, or a military vehicle to scrape a civilian car or truck. But in each of these cases there was a procedure to be followed to ensure that the injured party was made whole.

All in all the two years of maneuvers - bringing more than 850,000 new residents to the area even if only temporary - proved to be a period of economic prosperity for Lebanon, Wilson County, and the other participating counties.

It was also a time for romance and for many young maidens to find soulmates and marry. A number of the soldiers who came to the area for training returned after the war and became permanent citizens. Some married before they left, while others made promises of marriage and waited until their safe return before exchanging vows.

# Potpourri

*Where whites and blacks worshipped together*

Pickett Chapel is regarded as the oldest church building in Lebanon and one of the town's first brick structures.

In 1866, a group of former slaves bought the building located on the east side of Lebanon on East Market Street after it had been abandoned by a white congregation some ten years earlier.

The lot on which the church was built was purchased for $75 in 1812 by the Methodists. However, it wasn't until 1827 that a church was built on the site.

*Historic Pickett Chapel.*

History tells that both slaves and slave owners worshipped together at the church in the early years with slaves sitting in a balcony section and whites below on the main floor of the church.

It is reported in the Wilson County African American history book *In Their Own Voices* that "On July 18, 1866 some 30 of the black Methodists came together to discuss their concern about their spiritual welfare and the need for a place of their own to worship. It was decided they would purchase Seay Chapel, a vacant church on East Market Street. They had formerly worshipped there for many years with the white congregation."

The first pastor of the new congregation was Rev. Calvin Pickett for whom the church was named.

Pickett Chapel fell into a state of bad repair and the congregation meeting there had grown to the point that it needed a larger church in which to worship.

As a result, a new church, Pickett-Rucker Methodist Church, was built and opened in 1973 on Glover Street. The name Rucker was added to the church's name in honor of Rev. T.G. Rucker, who was the pastor of the congregation when the decision was made to build a new building.

On April 18, 1977, Pickett Chapel was inducted into the National Register of Historic Places.

In 2007 the Wilson County Black History Committee (WCBHC) purchased the building and began an ongoing restoration project.

*In the center of Lebanon's Square*

The statue honoring Brig. Gen. Robert Hopkins Hatton was erected in the center of Lebanon's Public Square on May 20, 1912 by the United Daughters of the Confederacy.

The son of a Methodist minister, Hatton was born in Steubenville, Ohio in 1826. His family moved to Tennessee in 1842. He studied law at Cumberland University and was admitted to the bar in 1850. In December 1852, he married Sophie K. Reilly of Williamson County. They had three children and the family lived in a house on West Main Street at the northeast corner of West Main and North Hatton Avenue.

He was elected to the state legislature in 1855 as a member of the Whig Party; ran an unsuccessful campaign for governor in 1857; and was elected to Congress in 1858 as an Opposition party candidate because the Whig party had become defunct. He was 32 when he began his time in Congress.

Hatton, who initially supported the preservation of the Union and opposed secession, reversed his position when President Lincoln in 1861 called for 75,000 volunteers to suppress unlawful actions in several southern states following the attack on Fort Sumter.

Reacting to Lincoln's call, Hatton formed a Confederate military unit, the Lebanon Blues, which became a part of the 7th Tennessee. He was subsequently elected as colonel of the regiment and the unit was deployed to western Virginia in July 1861.

Less than a year later, Hatton, who had served with distinction, was promoted on May 23, 1862 to Brigadier General of the 4th Brigade, 1st Division, Army of Northern Virginia.

On the evening of May 31, 1862, only eight days following his promotion, he died, as he led his troops of the Tennessee Brigade at the Battle of Seven Pines also recognized as the Battle of Fair Oaks in Henrico County, VA near Richmond. He was 35.

It's reported that he was last seen alive in the charge on Nine Mile Road, waving his hat, and cheering his men with his final words, "Forward, my brave boys! Forward!"

Hatton's body was returned to Knoxville for burial, because Middle Tennessee at the time was occupied by Federal troops. On March 23, 1866, he was reburied in Lebanon's Cedar Grove Cemetery.

Some 30 years following his death, Hatton's pistols were returned to his family by a Union soldier who had found them on the battlefield.

By the time of Gen. Lee's surrender at Appomattox on April 9, 1865, only 47 men of the original 1,000 soldiers who had joined Hatton from Wilson, Smith, Sumner and DeKalb counties had survived the war.

In his short 35 years of life Robert Hatton accomplished much. He had earned a degree in law, established a successful law practice, been elected to the state legislature and U.S. Congress, and served in the Confederacy as a Brigadier General.

His frequent letter writing to his wife during his time in public office in Nashville and Washington made it evident that to him his marriage and children were his proudest accomplishments.

*Battle fought in Lebanon*

While there were a number of significant Civil War battles fought near Lebanon at places like Hartsville, Franklin and Murfreesboro, history notes that Lebanon was the site of only one skirmish between troops of the North and South.

According to historical reports, Gen. Ebenezer Dumont of the Union Army was in pursuit of Col. John Hunt Morgan's Confederate Cavalry with a force from the Nashville Garrison when the Union general surprised Morgan in Lebanon on the morning of May 5, 1862.

Dumont launched his attack near dawn on Morgan's Cavalry that was camped around the Lebanon Square and at Cumberland University located at the time on South College Street.

Following Dumont's charge, a 15-mile running battle ensued in which Morgan and members of his unit were forced to retreat on routes east of Lebanon along Rome Pike and Trousdale Ferry Pike.

During the fighting Confederate sympathizers in Lebanon fired on the Union Cavalry soldiers.

Confederates who remained barricaded themselves inside buildings around the town's center and eventually surrendered when Dumont threatened to burn the town to the ground.

Dumont's force of some 600 men included detachments from the 1st Kentucky Cavalry commanded by Col. Frank Lane Wolford, the 4th Kentucky Cavalry commanded by Col. Green Clay Smith, and the 7th Pennsylvania Cavalry commanded by Col. George Wynkoop.

Morgan's force was the 2nd Kentucky Cavalry Regiment and was comprised of 800 troops.

As a result of the battle, 150 Confederates were taken prisoner and 60 were killed, while 10 Union soldiers were killed, 21 were wounded, and 5 were reported missing. The number of Confederate soldiers wounded or missing was not reported.

*Noted poet and humorist*

Dixon Merritt (1879 - 1972) served as Tennessee State Director of Public Safety, taught at Cumberland University and was editor of The Nashville Tennessean and The Lebanon Democrat newspapers. He was a contributor and editor of the "History of Wilson County" published in 1961.

In 1910 he gained national recognition with a limerick he authored about a pelican.

*A wonderful bird is the pelican,*
*His bill will hold more than his belican,*
*He can take in his beak*
*Enough food for a week*
*But I'm damned if I see how the helican*

*Pulitzer winner*

David Hall, from Lebanon, was a 1961 graduate of Castle Heights Military Academy and is credited for leading the Denver Post when its newsroom was awarded the Putlizer Prize Gold Medal for Meritorious Public Service in 1986.

Hall, who began his career in journalism at The Nashville Tennessean the day after his Heights graduation, had career stops at the Chicago Daily News and Chicago Sun-Times, as assistant managing editor; the Pioneer Press and the Dispatch in St. Paul, Minnesota, as managing editor and executive editor; the Denver Post as editor and senior vice president (1984-1988); as editor of the Bergen Record in New Jersey from 1988 to 1992; and editor of the Cleveland Plain Dealer.

Under his leadership, the Denver Post won the Pulitzer Prize Gold Medal for Meritorious Public Service in 1986.

*First a home for a governor, now a funeral home*

Robert Looney Caruthers moved to Lebanon after he received his license to practice law in 1824.

He won property on West Main Street in a raffle in 1826 and hired Henry Reiff, a native of Wilson County, to design and build a home on the land he had won. Reiff had just recently built The Hermitage, the home of President Andrew Jackson.

Caruthers' home was completed in 1828 and remains today as Ligon and Bobo Funeral Home.

Judge Caruthers was elected Governor of Tennessee in 1863, however he was never inaugurated, due to the fact that Tennessee was occupied by Union forces.

The Cumberland University Law School was founded in his law office in 1847, when he and his brother, Abraham, organized it with seven students. He was the first President of the Board of Trust and was professor of law at Cumberland from the time the school was reopened following the Civil War until his death in 1882.

*428 West Main Street*

One of Lebanon's most unique homes, a Queen-Anne style Victorian edifice, was built by Isaac William Pleasant (I.W.P.) Buchanan. Construction began on the home in 1894 and was completed in 1897.

Buchanan (1866-1943) came to Lebanon as a child when his father, Dr. A.H. Buchanan, accepted a teaching position at Cumberland University. Buchanan received his bachelor and doctorate degrees from Cumberland and served as professor of mathematics from

*IWP Buchanan House.*

1894-1898.

He held several patents, and in addition to being a founder of Castle Heights School in 1902, he also designed the school's Main Administration building.

The Buchanan home, once owned by Cracker Barrel founder Dan Evins, was listed on the National Register of Historic Places in 1979.

*Imperial Wizard shows-up here*

In the summer of 1980 the Ku Klux Klan targeted Lebanon and Wilson County.

For several weeks the KKK tormented the community with threats and staging appearances by heavily armed Klan members donned in white gowns and hoods proclaiming vows of white supremacy.

*KKK Imperial Wizard Bill Wilkinson speaks at a rally in Lebanon.*

Their appearance in Lebanon drew the ire of local government, businesses, and the citizenry in general. The Lebanon Democrat published a front page editorial denouncing the KKK and the Klan's efforts in Lebanon and Wilson County.

Bill Wilkinson, who held the title Imperial Wizard, was the national leader of the KKK and appeared in Lebanon at a Klan rally on Saturday, August 23, 1980. The local newspaper reported that between 300 and 400 attended the rally which was held in an open field off U.S. Hwy. 231 South near the I-40 intersection.

*One of the best in the South*

The Wilson County Fair has become not only one of the region's most popular fair's but arguably one of the South's with an annual attendance far above the half million mark and threatening 600,000.

This is a far cry from whence the first county fair was held in Lebanon and far exceeds the fair's record for several years when it was reorganized in 1979 under Wilson County Promotions, a nonprofit entity led by a handful of individuals who thought Wilson County deserves and should have a first-class blue-ribbon county fair.

The effort under the Wilson County Promotions tent was led by several businessmen, agricultural leaders and others. Among those who were cited with a great deal of the credit for reviving the fair were Randall Clemons, Johnny Trice, the late Hale Moss, Nelson Steed and others.

In a history about the Wilson County Fair written by the late Johnny Knowles and published in The Wilson Post, Knowles says the first known fair in Wilson County was held in 1853.

The location of the 1853 fair was on Coles Ferry Pike near where the Jimmy Floyd Center is located. The fair was held annually at this location, according to Knowles, until about 1884.

He writes that in 1919 a group of citizens organized and held a two-day fair on the Public Square with exhibits being housed in the Courthouse on the Square. This fair was so successful that a fair board was formed and land was acquired on Coles Ferry Pike, being the very same land used for previous fairs. This was considered to be the first local county fair of the 1900s.

*Wilson County Fair Logo.*

In 1920, a grandstand, stables and one cattle barn were erected at the fairgrounds and over 20,000 people attended the fair.

In 1927, all Confederate Veterans were admitted free during the Fair.

The 25th year for the fair was celebrated in 1944. Shortly after the fair had ended on Thursday night around 11 o'clock a fire destroyed the grandstands. A livestock sale had been held at the fairgrounds that afternoon and although the grandstands were a total loss, firefighters did manage to save the livestock barn which contained over $10,000 worth of livestock. Replacing the grandstands lost the year before, new larger grandstands were constructed in 1945.

In 1946 the fair set an attendance record with more than 12,000 in attendance on Friday night alone. Knowles notes, "There was good cause for celebration too. The war was over, the maneuvers were gone, and wartime restrictions had been lifted. The L. J. Heath Shows brought a big midway to the fair, featuring a giant military searchlight which, according to the show, could be seen for up to 100 miles."

In 1950, the big attraction for the fair was a television set.

The fair continued through the 1950s and was purchased by a new group of stockholders in the 1960s. The last year for the fair under the ownership of the new group was in 1969. From 1970 through 1972, there was no fair held in Wilson County.

In 1973, the Lebanon Jaycees revived the fair. The fair continued to be held on the Coles Ferry Pike property until 1974, when this property was sold at auction.

In 1974, a group of individuals met at the Farm Bureau office to organize a campaign to ask the county to purchase ten acres of the Baddour property on Sparta Pike in Lebanon. The Baddour estate, which was represented by Mayor Bill Baird, held approximately 104 acres at the Sparta Pike site. The group interested in acquiring the property was told by Baird that they could purchase either ten acres or all 104 acres.

*A woman and her grandson ride the swings at the Wilson County Fair.*

When the County Court met in March 1974, a member of the Court, Bob Burton, of LaGuardo, made the motion to purchase the entire 104-acre tract of the Baddour estate. The motion was seconded by Nathan Hankins, a Lebanon businessman who was a partner in the McClain and Smith men's apparel store on the Square. The motion passed, the entire 104-acre tract was purchased, and in 1975 the fair moved from Coles Ferry Pike to the new location named the James E. Ward Agricultural Center in honor of the long serving Wilson County Extension Agent. The Jaycees continued to sponsor the fair through 1978.

In 1979, Wilson County Promotions was formed and the first fair under its direction was held the same year. Attendance for this fair was reported to be 12,000.

Since 1979, the Wilson County Fair has grown by all measures. It's received numerous awards, been featured in regional and national publications, and attracts visitors from hundreds of miles away who book rooms in local hotels and stay in Lebanon so that they can attend the fair on multiple nights.

And largely because of the Wilson County Fair a number of improvements have been made to the Ward Agricultural Center, including the acquisition of additional acreage, construction of several buildings and arenas, and most recently the new Wilson County Exposition Center.

*Cutting grass with a string*

Before cutting grass with a nylon cord became so popular, Jack Cato's television shop on South Maple Street became the first retailer in Lebanon to sell Weed Eaters. Cato, a Korean War veteran and former Cracker Barrel board member, ran a series of newspaper advertisements in the late 1960s, about a quarter page in size, that convinced readers that this new contraption did indeed work and grass could be cut with a string.

Cato became one of Weed Eater's best dealers leading the southeast and much of the nation in sales.

# Potpourri

*Sherry's Run*

Annually Lebanon residents don mailboxes, front porches, some even the front of their cars with bright green colored bows. The bows are the symbol of Sherry's Run, a community-wide 5k Run/Walk held each year to raise money to aid those who are battling cancer.

Faith, courage, optimism and a desire to help others were qualities that defined Sharon "Sherry" Patterson Whitaker, who lost her battle with cancer in 2004 and in whose memory Sherry's Run is held. Gary Whitaker, Sherry's husband and local bank executive, seeing firsthand the struggles that cancer patients and their caretakers face, started the event shortly after her death.

A modest fundraiser in its early years, Sherry's Run now attracts hundreds of participants each year and is raising hundreds of thousands of dollars.

The organization's website states, "With God's blessings and immeasurable support from our community, Sherry's Run, has grown from a onetime 5K Run/Walk into a Christ centered, non-profit organization giving HOPE to families who are fighting cancer."

*Helping others*

Lebanon surgeon Dr. George Robertson, Sr., has made countless trips to deprived third world countries to provide much needed, life-saving medical aid.

A member of College Hills Church of Christ, Dr. Robertson, a practitioner for more than 50 years, began his service of providing medical aid and missionary work in remote countries when he would accompany the late Dr. Henry Farrar, also a member of the College Hills church, on mission trips.

*Feeding the hungry*

The late Bob and Peggy Evans gave up a successful furniture retail store, Town and Country Home Furnishings, that they owned on West Main Street, and followed their faith in 1996 to begin a new local ministry, Love One Another Embassy, Inc., a nonprofit entity originally focused on international missions and "feeding people physical and spiritual food" in countries around the world.

Three years later the couple, realizing that there was a significant need locally for their mission of feeding the hungry, began the Joseph's Storehouse Food Ministry.

Today Joseph's Storehouse helps feed as many as 500 families monthly. Among those served about 45 percent are elderly or disabled and 35 percent are single parents living below poverty level.

*Featured on Page 1 of The Wall Street Journal*

He served as chairman of the board at Lebanon's First Federal Savings and Loan Association until his death at age 107 and because of this most unusual feat he was featured on the front page of The Wall Street Journal.

Walter J. Baird, for whom a middle school in the Lebanon Special School District is named, took an airplane ride on his 100th birthday, was the oldest living active Rotarian in the world, and through his association with the home loan industry is credited with helping thousands of local young married couples own their own home.

Born near Baird's Mill on July 3, 1873, he grew up with ambitions to be a railway mail clerk and although he became qualified for such a position as he had passed the required Civil Service exam, his career path took a much different route.

He acquired and sold ownership interests in various retail stores, took a job as a bookkeeper, was hired as a bank cashier in 1914, went back into retail as the owner of a hardware store, and in 1934 became the office manager of the local savings and loan. He eventually became president of the savings and loan and when he retired from active business, he became the organization's board chairman.

He was a member of the 10th district school board (now the Lebanon Special School District) and a trustee of Cumberland University. He and his wife, Ethel Bouton Baird, donated the funds for the restoration of the chapel in Memorial Hall at Cumberland University. The chapel was renamed Baird Chapel in honor of the couple's gift.

Mr. Baird died on February 16, 1980.

*Giving the opportunity to live independently*

Largely through the efforts of Lebanon businessman T.A. Bryan, Cedarcroft Home, Inc., a facility dedicated to the care and welfare of the mentally handicapped, disadvantaged and homeless men, was established in 1974 and licensed by the Tennessee Department of Mental Health and Retardation in 1996.

Cedarcroft provides room and board, access to health care, and the opportunity for as many as 136 residents to live independently despite their personal challenges and disabilities.

The Cedarcroft facility is located on South College Street in what was formerly Martha Gaston Hospital.

*Not a hand-out but a hand-up*

Brooks Franklin showed up one morning at The Lebanon Democrat asking to be employed as a general assignment reporter in the early 1980s. He had a high school diploma, a few credit hours at a nearby community college, and his only writing experience came from him putting together a church bulletin on a weekly basis in Smith County, where he lived at the time.

He was hired.

His talent for reporting and his writing style were like natural gifts. He could ask hard questions, find the gut of a story, and was good at making subjects and verbs agree.

Despite his scraggly unkempt red hair, he always had the mannerisms to endear those with whom he associated, district attorneys, law enforcement, and often the downtrodden. Because his life was so complicated with a number of personal challenges, he could easily relate to others facing similar obstacles.

Before his untimely death he wrote a number of stories about the homeless in Wilson County that served to make the community better aware of the size and plight of this population and especially the need for temporary shelter for women and children.

Not long after his death, Community Homeless Outreach and Support, Inc., was established in 2006 and the name Brooks House was adopted by the nonprofit entity.

In March 2007 Liz Reese was hired as director of Brooks House and in July property at 219 Virginia Avenue was purchased to serve as its principle location.

A major renovation of the 2,700 sq. ft. facility was completed in April 2008 and Brooks House was officially opened to provide a safe, comfortable environment for women and children seeking shelter, and to connect them with resources to help change their lives.

Brooks House strives to provide the women it serves with a hand-up, not a hand-out and to give them a chance to make different lives for themselves and their children.

*Not just a place to sell cattle*

In 1935, the late Jim Johnson, a farmer, cattleman, banker, real estate broker, businessman, and former City of Lebanon council member, opened the Sale Barn otherwise recognized as the Wilson County Livestock Market.

"Mr. Jim's" venture, located just off West Main Street on Rocky Road initially, was a mainstay in the buying and selling of livestock in Middle Tennessee for more than 75 years.

After Johnson's introduction the business had other owners including

Sam Andrews, Bill Talley, B.D. Atwood, E.B. Woodard and Fisher Smith.

For more than 25 years Alvin McKee, a member of the Wilson County Agricultural Hall of Fame, owned and operated the Sale Barn. He first became associated with the business in 1950 when it moved from its first location to a new facility on West Main Street on a site adjacent to what today is generally recognized as the Kroger Shopping Center.

Under McKee's ownership the Wilson County Livestock Market became a family business with his sons Bill and Carson McKee taking an active role along with his daughter, Wanda Bates. On the McKees' watch the Sale Barn became more than just a place for area cattlemen to bring their stock to be auctioned.

Before there was a Hardee's, McDonald's or even a Driver's (now Clayborn's) Bakery, the Sale Barn restaurant was the place to go for an early morning breakfast to get caught up on current events and local politics. The place was filled each morning with a diversified crowd of patrons, some wearing overalls and boots and others in dark suits and neckties.

In the spring of 2009, the McKees made the decision to close the Sale Barn. The last livestock auction was held there on June 3. Since its closing the Sale Barn has been torn down and the property cleared.

*Lebanon civic/service clubs*

The Lebanon Rotary Noon Club, chartered in 1921, was the first civic/service club to be organized in the community. In 1933 the Lebanon Lions Club was chartered followed by the Lebanon Kiwanis in 1946. A second Rotary Club, the Lebanon Breakfast Rotary was chartered in 1989.

*Did you know*
- Ft. Campbell, home of the 101st Airborne, is named after Gov. Bowen Campbell who lived in Lebanon.

## Notes from Lebanon's First 200 Years

- Two justices of the U.S. Supreme Court graduated from Cumberland University's Law School, Justice Howell Edmunds Jackson and Justice Horace Harmon Lurton.

- Sam Houston, a Tennessee governor and hero at the Alamo, lived in Lebanon for a short while and practiced law in an office at 109 East Main Street.

- Cumberland University's Law School was sold to Samford University in Birmingham, Ala. for $125,000 in 1961.

- William Bowen Campbell, who lived on Coles Ferry Pike in Lebanon (the Campbell home remains directly across from the entrance to the Lebanon Country Club) was elected governor in 1851.

- James Chamberlain "Lean Jimmy" Jones, who lived in Lebanon near the intersection of U.S. Hwy. 231 North and Hartmann Drive (the Jones home remains on this site today), twice served as governor and twice defeated James K. Polk to become governor. Jones later served as a U.S. Senator.

- Robert Caruthers, from Lebanon, was elected governor in 1863 but never was allowed to take office because federal troops occupied the state.

- Georgia Tech beat Cumberland University in football in 1916 by a score of 222-0, which still stands as a record defeat in college football. John Heisman was Tech's coach. The book about the game, "Heisman's First Trophy," explains that Cumberland didn't have a football team in 1916 but was forced into playing the game by Heisman and Tech or face a breach of contract lawsuit.

Potpourri

*Cumberland football team that played Georgia Tech in 1916.*

- Tater Peeler road, on Lebanon's south side, was originally called Sinking Creek Road. However, the road was renamed Tater Peeler Road around 1890 when a farmer hauling a trailer load of potatoes into Lebanon on the rough unfinished rocky road found his load to be skinned and somewhat peeled upon his arrival.

- U.S. Secretary of State Cordell Hull, father of the United Nations, was a graduate of Cumberland University. Hull, who served as Secretary of State during World War II, held the position longer than anyone else.

- Lebanon's oldest car dealership, Wilson County Motors, was founded in 1927 by Winstead Paine Bone, Jr. and A.W. Hooker. Other partners in the dealership have included Dee Manning, Sam Hopkins, Mort Harkey, and Dan Denney. Ownership in the dealership remains today in W.P. Bone, III's family. The dealership offers for sale Chevrolet, Buick, GMC, & Hyundai brands.

- The Lebanon Post Office in 1848 was one of only seven in Tennessee to handle the 1947 issue of postage stamps, the first ever produced by the U.S. government.

*Seeing things they can't explain*

Before the abbreviation for an Unidentified Flying Object became so generally known, reports of residents in Lebanon seeing UFOs were documented in the local newspaper and in other records including the "History of Wilson County."

The National UFO Reporting Center cites several sightings in Lebanon, the earliest being in 1972.

But there were other UFO reports here before 1972. Several UFO sightings are noted in the "History of Wilson County." Those mentioned occurred in the 1950s.

A 1995 telephone call to the Tennessee Emergency Management Agency relating what a mom and her daughter witnessed got a great deal of attention locally.

According to TEMA, a woman in Lebanon called and said she and her daughter had witnessed "multiple ships near Cainesville Road, two large ones and several smaller, white ones."

The woman reported that at 6:25 a.m. "the white ones were seen suddenly to gather around the big ones. The last smaller ship was red."

Colors observed during the sighting based on the TEMA report were red, blue, blue-green, and white. The witness said what she saw looked like "beautiful clamshells." She said when the objects moved, they bobbed up and down, and in every other direction. "When they departed, they moved very fast, and left a visible tail that looked like a baseball bat," she concluded.

The sighting occurred on January 24, 1995 and lasted for 108 minutes. There actually are 11 instances dating back to 1972 in which UFO reports in Lebanon are recorded by the National UFO Reporting Center.

The latest sighting reported occurred on June 14, 2018.

According to the witness, he was driving East on I-40 "headed back home to Lebanon from work. As I was driving, I look to my left and saw an object just sitting in the sky. It was brown in color and its shape was a long thin cylinder with what appeared to be windows down the length of the side.

"It was stationary, but then it shot off to the East (same direction I was traveling) and flew in to a cloud and did not come out the other side which did not make sense because at the rate it was traveling it should have appeared on the other side of the cloud in about three seconds after entering.

"I watched the cloud for some time, until it became impossible for me to turn my head back in that direction any longer."

*Two area resorts*

The name Hamilton Springs is likely familiar to many current readers as the residential and commercial development underway on U.S. Hwy. 70 just west of town. Announced at its beginning as the first transit-oriented development in Tennessee, the farm on which the project is rapidly taking shape is owned by the Charles Bell family and is being developed by brothers Jack and Rick Bell.

Already in place is a single family residential section, a major apartment complex, a commercial office and retail building, and opened on site in 2018 was a Music City Star commuter rail stop. Construction has begun on a senior living facility and additional plans call for more residential options blended with commercial and retail amenities.

The development is described as a long-range project.

Before this Hamilton Springs there was another.

Advertised in 1912 as being only four miles from Lebanon, the Hamilton Springs of this period was a resort complete with a hotel and located on the Tennessee Central Railroad to be convenient for guests arriving from Nashville or other communities connected to passenger rail service.

According to the advertisement, "The hotel at this beautiful resort is surrounded by a grove of beautiful forest trees, and Mr. J. W. Hamilton, the genial proprietor, spares no effort in attending to the comfort of his guests."

Also in 1912 there was another resort four miles from Lebanon, Horn Springs, a competitor to Hamilton Springs.

Horn Springs was also adjacent to the Tennessee Central Railroad and featured a resort style hotel and other attractions for its guests.

After the Horn Springs hotel closed it was purchased years later and the property's owner in the 1950s, Dr. Dean Wilkinson, a Lebanon dentist, operated a public swimming pool on the site. It was also a popular place for picnics, dance parties and summer social gatherings. The property today is owned by the Bell family.

*First private 18-hole course*

In 1999, a 505 acre cattle farm located on U.S. Hwy. 70 and owned by Bascom Cooksey, Jr., was sold in one tract and plans were soon orchestrated for a first-of-its-kind lifestyle community for Lebanon.

The development, Five Oaks, today includes an 18-hole championship golf course that was opened in 2001, single family homes, villas, paired patio homes, and upscale multi-family housing along with some 40 acres of commercial property that will have accessibility to the Music City Star commuter rail service. When completed the residential community, including all components, will contain approximately 1,000 rooftops.

The all private Five Oaks Country Club and Golf Course features oversized bent grass greens and zoysia fairways and a 21,000 sq. ft. clubhouse resting atop one of Lebanon's highest ridges and provides for its members and their guests stunning panoramic views looking into neighboring Trousdale, Macon and Smith counties, and the foothills of southern most Kentucky.

*Highlander founder Cumberland graduate*

Myles Horton, founder of the Highlander Folk School in Monteagle (now Highlander Research and Education Center), a once controversial academy that focused its teachings on how best to empower adults for social change, was a 1928 graduate of Cumberland University.

Horton, from Savannah, started Highlander School in 1932 and remained its director until 1973.

He left his rural West Tennessee home at age 15 to attend high school and to begin working hard labor jobs in order to earn money to pay college tuition. He enrolled at Cumberland in 1924.

The term "communist" was applied to Horton's teachings and the Highlander School because of the school's philosophy of bringing whites and blacks together, in violation of segregation laws. The school advocated for the working class and the poor. Rosa Parks was heavily influenced by Myles Horton and the Highlander School. Just prior to her famous refusal to give up her seat on a bus, Parks attended Highlander School and accredited her time at Highlander for giving her the courage to protest.

Other prominent leaders of the civil rights movement were influenced by Highlander including Dr. Martin Luther King, Jr., U.S. Rep. John Lewis, James Bevel, Bernard Lafayette, Ralph Abernathy, John B. Thompson and many others.

Dr. King spoke at the school in 1957 on its 25th anniversary praising Horton and Highlander. An undercover agent sent by the Georgia Commission on Education took a photograph of King. The photo was sent throughout the South and used as a propaganda tool against King, with claims that it showed him attending a Communist training school.

Notes from Lebanon's First 200 Years

The Highlander Research and Education Center has been located in New Market, Tenn. in Jefferson County since 1971. Highlander currently focuses its activity on democratic participation and economic justice with a particular focus on youth, immigrants to the U.S. from Latin America, African Americans, LGBT, and economically deprived white people.

*Important Dates*
1802 - Town of Lebanon laid out; lots sold at auction.
1803 - First county jail built. Located on Public Square.
1808 - First meeting of commissioners.
1814 - First patrol appointed.
1818 - Lebanon Gazette, town's first newspaper opens.
1819 - Town of Lebanon Chartered.
1823 - Use of Town Spring regulated.
1823 - Wooden chimneys forbidden.
1830 - Fire company organized.
1842 - Cumberland University opens.
1850 - Lebanon pop. 1,554.
1866 - Former slaves purchase Pickett Chapel Church.
1867 - Fakes and Hooker Lumber Company opens.
1867 - African Americans given right to vote.
1870 - Lebanon pop. 2,073.
1876 - First black, a shoemaker from Lebanon, elected to County Court.
1890 - Lebanon pop. 1,883.
1897 - 458 telephones in Lebanon.
1882 - First phone lines between Lebanon and Nashville.
1900 - Lebanon pop. 1,956.
1901 - State Legislature creates Lebanon Special School District.
1902 - Castle Heights Military Academy opens.
1908 - Lebanon Woolen Mills established.
1910 - Lebanon's population was 3,659.
1913 - Post Office on East Main opened. Now County Election Commission.
1916 - Cumberland loses to Georgia Tech in football 222-0.
1917 - Lebanon buys first fire engine.
1919 - First airplane to land in Wilson County lands in Lebanon.
1920 - Lebanon pop. 4,084.
1924 - City okays concrete paving of major city streets.

## Potpourri

1924 - Lebanon Chamber of Commerce organized.
1930 - Lebanon pop. 4,656.
1932 - Water from Cumberland River flows into city pipes.
1939 - Mule sales on Public Square prohibited.
1940 - Lebanon pop. 5,950.
1942 - Automatic railroad crossing signals replace watchmen.
1946 - First parking meters installed.
1946 - Wilson County Colored Fair Association holds first fair.
1950 - Lebanon pop. 7,915.
1951 - Winter of the "Great Ice Storm."
1953 - City consumers begin using natural gas.
1956 - West Main Street widened to four lanes.
1957 - Southern Bell converts to dial phones.
1960 - Lebanon pop. 10,512.
1961 - Cumberland sells Law School to Samford University in Birmingham, AL.
1963 - New City Hall opened on College Street.
1964 - James Bryant was first African American teacher at Lebanon High School.
1964 - Hattie Bryant (wife of James Bryant) becomes first black teacher at Lebanon Junior High.
1969 - I-40 opened from Nashville to east side of Cumberland County.
1969 - Cracker Barrel Old Country Store restaurant chain launched.
1970 - Lebanon pop. 12,492.
1977 - Groundbreaking for UMC Hospital.
1980 - Lebanon pop. 11,872.
1982 - Historic West Side Hotel burns.
1986 - Castle Heights Military Academy closes.
1989 – Valentine's Day flood claims a life.
1990 - Lebanon pop. 15,208.
1992 - Cumberland's Rudy Nursing School opens.
2000 - Lebanon pop. 20,235.
2006 - Music City Star begins rail commuter service from Lebanon to Nashville.
2010 - City suffers major flooding. Storm said to be 1,000 year flood.
2010 - Lebanon pop. 26,190.
2012 - New Lebanon High School is opened.
2018 - Lebanon pop. following special census 35,050.
2019 - UMC hospital sells to Vanderbilt Medical Center.

# Chapter Eleven
## Which Would You Choose?

So, if you were in Chicago and met a stranger while eating lunch and he says to you, "I can tell you're from the South by the way you ordered your BLT, but I can't decide from the accent if it's Tennessee or Georgia. Which is it?"

You answer, "Tennessee."

Next question from your new friend met over a bowl of soup and a BLT, "Where about in Tennessee?"

"A small town about 30 miles east of Nashville, Lebanon," is your response.

Now the conversation turns to one of those "small world" type of things when your new friend says, "Oh yeah. I know about Lebanon. That's where _____ ."

You fill-in the blank.

What are three items for which Lebanon is most famous? There are a lot of options to consider.

Quaker Oats chose a Lebanon resident in 1947 to play the role of Aunt Jemima to promote a number of its products.

W.E.B. Du Bois, a founder of the NAACP and first African American to receive a doctorate degree from Harvard, lived in Lebanon for one summer while earning a teacher's certificate.

The Second Army headquarters was based in Lebanon while more than 800,000 troops trained in Middle Tennessee for combat in Europe during World War II.

Toshiba, a Japanese company, built its first manufacturing facility in the Western Hemisphere in Lebanon.

# Notes from Lebanon's First 200 Years

A number of famous songwriters and country music artists live or have lived in or near Lebanon.

This list represents some very good candidates for Lebanon's most memorable or best known assets but three that tend to standout more than others include Cumberland University, Cracker Barrel Old Country Store, Inc., and Castle Heights Military Academy.

*Cumberland University*

In the early 1980s a community survey was conducted in Dickson County. Among the survey questions asked was what feature or amenity did Dickson County need that it didn't have at the time.

The answer that gained the single most responses was a four-year university.

Dickson County is not alone in its thinking. A lot of communities would like to have a four-year university sitting two blocks from their Public Square.

Since 1942, Cumberland has been a formidable asset to Lebanon.

Sure, it has had its challenges dating back to when the first administration building was burned to the ground in 1864 by what many reports say was an act by Union troops.

But Cumberland has a distinguished national reputation and has far more to its credit than the ugly defeat a bunch of fraternity boys suffered to Georgia Tech in football in 1916. (If you don't recall, Cumberland lost by what is still a college football record score, 222-0.)

Cumberland's contributions have been many. Few universities can boast about having among their alumni a U.S. Secretary of State, two justices of the U.S. Supreme Court, scores of U.S. Congressmen, 14 state governors, three U.S. ambassadors, business leaders, and hundreds of others who have become college presidents, served in the judiciary or who have been respected public servants in state and local government.

The private independent university today offers more than 100 different degree programs for undergraduate studies and eight graduate degree areas of study.

Dr. Paul Stumb, who was inaugurated as Cumberland's 27th president in 2015, has led the university to consecutive record enrollments attracting students from all 50 states and dozens of foreign countries. The enrollment for fall 2019 is expected to be near the 2,600 mark.

*Cracker Barrel Old Country Store, Inc.*

In 1969, two good friends, who 50 years later would prove to be visionaries, had an idea.

"Let's put a family style restaurant near the interstate (I-40 from Nashville to Knoxville was completed in 1968 and from Nashville to Memphis in 1966) because lots of families are going to be traveling on these new highways and they're going to be looking to buy meals at a price they can afford and will need gas to fill-up their vehicles," was the scheme they conceived.

The late Dan Evins and Tommy Lowe combined their talents and resources with helping hands from several local townspeople and built the first Cracker Barrel off Hwy. 109 near I-40 in Lebanon.

Evins and Lowe recruited ten others to join them in their venture requiring each to put up $10,000. In return the ten became the restaurant

*Cracker Barrel's first restaurant at Leeville Pike and Hwy. 109 opened in 1969.*

chain's first board of directors along with Evins and Lowe. The original ten included Eddie Evins, Jack Cato, Ken Lester Jr., Buster Jennings, Don Irwin, Bill Heydel, Dr. Jim Bradshaw, Charles Simpson, John Shankle and Glenn Chaffin.

Bingo!

Their idea was an instant success. Soon after the first Cracker Barrel, there was a second and a third and so on. As of August 2019, there were 660 Cracker Barrel locations in 45 states. Along the way there were changes in strategies such as removing the gas pumps from each location and adding gift shops but all-in-all the concept has remained the same.

In 1981, the local ownership took the company public in order to raise capital for expansion opportunities. First shares of the stock were traded on the NASDAQ exchange at 60 cents per share. As recently as 2018, the

*A group of locals board a bus bound for Miami to see Tennessee play Oklahoma in the 1968 Orange Bowl. Waiting to board are Tommy Lowe, Martha Bradshaw, Bobbie Jane Lowe, Jimmy Draper, Jr., Barbara Miller, Dr. Gordon Miller, Cynthia Reed, Philip Reed, and Dr. Jim Bradshaw. The bus was owned by Dan Evins Shell Oilers professional softball team. Supposedly the highlight of the trip was the bus being able to crash the Orange Bowl parade. Evins and Lowe were co-founders of Cracker Barrel and Miller and Bradshaw were original board members.*

stock traded as high as $181.94 per share.

In 2011, Cracker Barrel stock could be bought for about $28 per share. A thousand shares of the restaurant chain's stock purchased in 2011 and valued at $28,000 would have been worth more than $175,000 on July 31, 2019.

While there have been a number of management changes, some things never change at Cracker Barrel. Their sausage still comes from the Purnell family, their bread from Bay Bread in Lebanon, and their turnip greens are still simmered with country ham.

Cracker Barrel reports that each year they serve about 217 million guests, 200 million biscuits, 160 million eggs, 135 million slices of bacon, and 57 million pancakes.

The company's headquarters is located in Lebanon on Hartmann Drive. Sandra B. Cochran has served as president and chief executive officer since September 2011.

*Castle Heights Military Academy*

At one time hundreds of cadets, ranging in age from 6 to 18, filled the ranks of a prestigious private military school, Castle Heights Military Academy, in Lebanon.

From the time of the school's opening in 1902 until its closing 80 years later in 1986, Castle Heights attracted students, cadets as they would become to be known, from virtually every state and several foreign countries.

The military academy was located on West Main Street a mile or so west of Lebanon's Public Square.

At one time after the mid-1950s when the school was reaching its pinnacle of popularity the cadet corps was comprised of close to 600 students representing grades one through twelve.

Founders of Castle Heights included Dr. David Mitchell, a former president of Cumberland University, Isaac W. P. Buchanan, a mathematics professor, A. W. Hooker, a Lebanon businessman, and Dr. Laban L. Rice, an English professor and also a former Cumberland president.

Originally the school was coeducational but became an all male military preparatory school in 1918 as a result of World War I. In 1970, facing significant decreases in enrollment, the administration and board of directors made the decision to once again accept female students.

The Vietnam War is blamed for Castle Heights and other schools of its kind for losing enrollment and eventually closing as the military became less and less popular.

The once prominent military school on "The Hill" in Lebanon closed in 1986.

Listed among the school's more famous alumni are Gregg and Duane Allman, founders of the Allman Brothers Band; Lt. Gen. John A. Bradley, U.S. Air Force, Commander of U.S. Air Force Reserve Command; Gen. Wesley Clark, U.S. Army and presidential candidate; Dan Evins, co-

*Cadets at Castle Heights Military Academy are inspected.*

## Which Would You Choose?

founder Cracker Barrel Old Country Store, Inc.; Gen. Lance Lord, U.S. Air Force, Commander of the Air Force Space Command; Pete Rademacher, heavyweight boxer; Herbert S. Walters, U.S. Senator from Tennessee; and John Wyeth Chandler, mayor of Memphis.

*Sunday afternoon parade in dress whites.*

# Acknowledgements

*Credits/Sources:*
Cumberland University; Cumberland University *Phoenix Rising;* *"History of Wilson County"*; *In Their Own Voices, An Account Of The Presence Of African Americans in Wilson County*; *The Lebanon Democrat*; *The Wilson Post*; *The Tennessean*; Tennessee Historical Marker; Lebanon Special School District; Friendship Christian School; *Heisman's First Trophy*; *Goodspeed's History of Tennessee by Counties*; Sloan, Eugene, *With Second Army, Somewhere in Tennessee*; McMillin, Woody, *In the Presence of Soldiers, The 2nd Army Maneuvers & Other World War II Activity in Tennessee*. Horton Heights Press, 2010; National Oceanic and Atmospheric Administration, Lebanon-Wilson County Chamber of Commerce; I.W.P Buchanan photos; and Col. J.B. Leftwich, Castle Heights Military Academy photos.

*Members of the City of Lebanon Bicentennial Committee:*
Rick Bell, City Historian
Sarah Haston, City of Lebanon ECD director
Debbie Jessen, City of Lebanon executive assistant
Melanie Minter, President, Lebanon-Wilson County Chamber of Commerce
Kim Parks, Executive Director, Historic Downtown Lebanon
Gwen Scott, Director, Fiddlers Grove
Bernie Ash, Mayor, City of Lebanon

*Ex-officio Committee members:*

| | |
|---|---|
| Amy Nichols | Britney Wilkerson |
| Cindy Yahola | David Hale |
| Emily Gannon | Shari Bazydola |
| Xavier Smith | Sam Hatcher |
| Jerry McFarland | George Coleman |
| Jared Felkins | Lanny Jewell |
| Linda Grandstaff | Marry Harris |
| Rob Hosier | Susan Hosier |

Made in the USA
Lexington, KY
20 December 2019